LIFE
Beyond
THE GRAVE

Christian Interfaith Perspectives

ALONZO L. GASKILL &
ROBERT L. MILLET, EDITORS

RSC
BYU

DESERET
BOOK

Published by the Religious Studies Center, Brigham Young University, Provo, Utah, in cooperation with Deseret Book Company, Salt Lake City.

Visit us at rsc.byu.edu.

Printed in the United States of America by Sheridan Books, Inc.

DESERET BOOK is a registered trademark of Deseret Book Company. Visit us at DeseretBook.com.

Cover and interior design by Emily V. Strong

ISBN: 978-1-9443-9469-1

Library of Congress Control Number: 2019936533

CONTENTS

ACKNOWLEDGMENTS

We gratefully acknowledge BYU Religious Education for sponsoring the "Beyond the Grave" conference and for each of the presenters for their remarkable contributions. We express appreciation to the Religious Studies Center team for their assistance: publications directors Thomas A. Wayment and Scott C. Esplin; publications coordinator Joany O. Pinegar; editors R. Devan Jensen, Emily Cook, Sharai McGill, and Petra Javadi-Evans; production supervisor Brent R. Nordgren; and designer Emily V. Strong.

INTRODUCTION

Robert L. Millet

Robert L. Millet is a professor emeritus of ancient scripture, Brigham Young University.

Surely no subject has captured the attention of men and women like that of death and the life beyond. Millions have sought with Job to know, "If a man die, shall he live again?" (Job 14:14). And if there is a future state, what is its nature? How best may mortal men and women prepare for it? Indeed, death has ever remained life's most awesome mystery. In the absence of revelation or divine guidance, humankind's would-be gaze into future worlds is unable to penetrate the darkness of the grave.

There is nothing more universal in this life than death; it is the common lot of all who come into this life to leave it. Every man or woman is born, and every man or woman must die. All are born as helpless infants, and all depart this sphere equally helpless in the face of death. Even among those who read by the lamp of religious under-standing, death is frequently viewed with fear and trembling. And why do we fear death? For some of us, it is because of our ignorance of the unknown, the anxiety associated with going to a place we do not under-stand. Others fear because they do know enough about what lies ahead and fret over a profligate lifestyle and the divine justice that awaits them. Others stew over unfinished earthly business. Even those who have lived lives that could be described as decent and upright are hesitant to let go, to surrender themselves to the powers of eternity and release their grip on time. Surely a God who has power over all things, even death, would be merciful enough to his children to reveal sufficient truth to prepare and comfort us concerning what lies ahead.

This book contains perspectives on life after death, primarily from selected proceedings of an academic conference held on the campus of Brigham Young University in March 2016. The title of the conference was "Beyond the Grave: Christian Interfaith Perspectives." Representatives of several professing Christian groups were asked to address the topics of death and what lies beyond death from the vantage point of their particular religious tradition. There has been no effort whatsoever to ignore theological differences between the various traditions, nor was it ever expected that a presenter compromise in the slightest what he or she holds to be true. This conference has been an ecumenical endeavor only in the sense that we came together to listen, to learn, to ask questions and inquire, in short, to better understand one another. In a world that is overrun with misunderstanding, misrepresentation, name-calling, and pigeonholing, nothing should be more welcome than understanding. At a time in our world's history when incivility and disrespect are the order of the day, a small group of religious-minded individuals met to have their perspectives expanded, their erroneous notions corrected and set aside, and their empathy and appreciation for those who are different from themselves enhanced.

Throughout the conference, we sought to embody what Professor Richard J. Mouw of Fuller Theological Seminary has described as "convicted civility."[1] It is a marvelous thing to discover a person who is deeply convicted about the tenets and practices of his or her faith. It is also an exciting occasion when differing parties treat one another in a civil manner. And it is a sheer delight to witness a person who is both convicted and civil.

It is our hope that readers will find the contents of this work to be both intellectually challenging and spiritually uplifting.

NOTE

1. Richard J. Mouw, *Uncommon Decency: Christian Civility in an Uncivil World*, rev. ed. (Downers Grove, IL: InterVarsity Press, 2010).

Chapter 1

DOGMA AND HYPOTHESIS

Purgatory, Limbo, and Catholic Views of the Afterlife

Mathew N. Schmalz

Mathew N. Schmalz, a Roman Catholic scholar, is a professor of religion at the College of Holy Cross in Worcester, Massachusetts.

I. FATHER/SON DISCUSSIONS

I grew up in a Roman Catholic family, and we fancied ourselves to be Catholics of an intellectual sort. The exception to this was my grandmother who was a Catholic of a more traditional kind and would often say the rosary by my bedside as I went to sleep.[1] Our family never fully integrated itself into the devotional rhythms that, in the 1960s and 1970s, still characterized what might be described as "ethnic Catholic life." My father was a college art professor and a Catholic convert, and I never saw him reciting a rosary, though tears would often fill his eyes when he discussed the mosaics of the Church of San Vitale in Ravenna or baroque church altars of Bernini. Given our intellectual propensities—or pretensions—it was a fairly regular practice for my father and me to have after-dinner discussions about theological questions such as the existence of God, the authenticity of papal authority, and the efficacy of Catholic sacraments.

During these father-and-son religious conversations, which, more often than not, would culminate in thinking through Catholic understandings of the afterlife, my father would often say to me, in a way both professorial and paternal, "You know, Mathew, your mother is a saint—she's going straight to heaven. But me," my dad would say, "I'm probably going to have to spend some time in purgatory"—referring to that intermediate place of "purgation" between earthly life and heavenly glory. The prospect of going there after death was a real possibility that evoked feelings of both fear and hope for life beyond the grave.

Our discussion of purgatory often would lead to considering another more theologically challenging aspect of the afterlife that had to do with the circumstances of my birth. I was an adopted child, so I spent the first four months of my life in an orphanage. I knew very little about my birth parents, but one thing I did know is that my birth mother had me baptized. My father, commenting again in a way both professorial and paternal, said, "Wasn't it thoughtful that your birth mother had you baptized? What if you had died before we had adopted you? You might have gone to limbo." Limbo was that place for infants who had never sinned but also never received the sacrament of baptism. I often imagined limbo as a warm, temperate place where it was always twilight: its inhabitants floated, surrounded by otherworldly ether.

Orthodox Christians do not accept the existence of purgatory, and limbo has also remained an exclusively Catholic concept. Taken together, however, purgatory and limbo often serve as evidence of the distinctiveness of Catholic doctrines concerning the afterlife: rigorously reasoned within a sophisticated and substantive tradition of theological inquiry in the view of some; idiosyncratic and unscriptural in the opinion of others.[2] For many non-Catholics, the most familiar representation of purgatory and limbo is that of Dante Alighieri's, who envisioned the minute details and geography of both realms in his allegorical *Divine Comedy*.[3] Dante positioned limbo at the uppermost level of hell; it is where virtuous pagans and unbaptized infants go. Dante likened purgatory to a mountain that is climbed in the process of human spiritual growth: at its summit, the gates of paradise open.

In the *Divine Comedy*, Dante extrapolated his vision from Catholic doctrine. But it is important to remember that limbo and purgatory have never been formally considered to be places in time and space as conventionally understood. Purgatory is a foundational point of Catholic doctrine that speaks to salvation as process of purification. By contrast, limbo is a kind of intellectual placeholder, a hypothesis that emphasizes the importance of baptism as a prerequisite for the beatific vision of heaven.

In the following discussion, we will more deeply explore Catholic understandings of the afterlife as reflected in the dogma of purgatory and the hypothesis of limbo. It is important to make the distinction between "dogma" and "hypothesis" here at the outset: not all ideas within the Catholic tradition have equal weight or claim equal measures of obedience. A dogma, simply put, is a divinely revealed truth, and it can reasonably be argued—with due respect given to dissenting views—that purgatory has the status of a divinely revealed truth when considered in light of its place within the Catholic tradition.[4] Limbo has another status entirely, and recently Pope Benedict XVI argued that limbo as a concept could be fruitfully discarded as a hypothesis that no longer aided Catholic considerations of the existence that follows death.[5] In considering purgatory and limbo together, we can learn much about Catholic understandings of the afterlife, the nature and progression of Catholic doctrine as a whole, and how Catholic doctrine can have a flexibility and plasticity that runs counter to conventional perceptions of it as rigid, unchanging, and, perhaps, unforgiving.[6]

II. DOGMA AND HYPOTHESIS

Recognizing the different doctrinal valences of purgatory and limbo—one a dogma and the other a hypothesis—turns us first to the overall edifice, or framework, of Catholic teaching, which has quite extensive and well-defined levels of authority. The sources of Catholic doctrine are scripture and tradition. Scripture as a source, in this case meaning the New Testament and the Hebrew Bible, should be clear enough and familiar to all Christians. But for Catholics, tradition stands alongside scripture as a basis for defining and developing doctrine. Tradition refers to the life and teaching of the Church and, together with scripture, constitutes an essential mode for transmitting revelation and the elements of faith.

It is the Magisterium—the "teaching authority"—of the Church that ensures the appropriate transmission and interpretation of elements of faith while articulating or prescribing their binding nature.[7] This teaching authority is granted to bishops and to the Pope, as the successor of the apostle Peter. It is important to understand that the Catholic Church does not see its teaching authority as somehow adding something new to revelation or as existing as revelation in its own right. Instead the Church believes that, as the Catechism of the Catholic Church, a compendium of Catholic doctrine, states, "The Magisterium is not superior to the Word of God, but its servant."[8] Accordingly, the Magisterium refers to an ability and authority to understand and teach the truths found explicitly and implicitly in tradition and scripture: an ability and authority that is understood as a "charism," an extraordinary gift of the Holy Spirit. Within the Catholic tradition, the Magisterium possesses what Avery Cardinal Dulles describes as a "threefold office" that involves not just teaching but sanctifying and ruling.[9]

The Magisterium as the teaching authority of the Church has two basic divisions: Sacred and Ordinary. The Sacred Magisterium teaches infallibly, either through specifically defined pronouncements of the pope or through a council approved by the pope. Doctrines proclaimed infallibly are called dogmas and require the assent of the faithful.[10] A relatively new category of teaching is called "definitive," which is of lesser authority but still requires obedient adherence.[11] The Ordinary Magisterium also contains teachings that are considered to be infallible if they are taught universally, but it contains nondefinitive and potentially fallible teachings as well. The rubric of fallible teachings would most certainly contain various theological hypotheses. And so, the Ordinary Magisterium may contain various speculations, which are changed, discarded, or proven wrong over time.

If you speak to most Catholics, you will find that few are aware of these distinctions. It's also important to note that other Catholic scholars and theologians might present or delineate the levels of Catholic doctrine differently than I have.[12] But suffice it to say, there is a great deal of complexity and nuance to Catholic thinking about doctrine. Although I may have outlined what seems to be a clear enough taxonomy of doctrine, in practice there is general ignorance about these standards, and in scholarly discourse there is much debate about what particular doctrine goes where, not to mention about the degree of change or development permitted as a doctrine persists through time.

III. A PROCESS OF PURGATION

Within Catholic doctrine, the idea of hell—eternal punishment sometimes envisioned as terrible heat and thirst—has longed seemed to stand uncomfortably alongside the belief that God is both loving and merciful. Noted German theologian Hans Urs von Balthasar wrote one of his most compact, and most discussed, books under the title *Dare We Hope That "All Men Be Saved."*[13] Balthasar said yes, we must dare and hope that all are saved, although he was distinguishing that hope from a doctrinal surety that all will be saved. Jesuit theologian Karl Rahner articulated his theory of the "anonymous Christian" to explain how even non-Christians may still attain salvation. According to Rahner, the grace of God exists as a fundamental constituent of human nature, and even non-Christian individuals who radically obey the dictates of their own consciences pertain to the Church, and to Jesus, as anonymous Christians.[14]

Given Balthasar's and Rahner's guarded optimism about the possibility of salvation, purgatory exists as an important possibility when considering what awaits the individual soul after death. The Catechism of the Catholic Church explains, "Each man receives his eternal retribution in his immortal soul at the very moment of his death, in a particular judgment that refers his life to Christ: either entrance into the blessedness of heaven—through a purification or immediately—or immediate and everlasting damnation."[15] Purgatory is that purification, which serves to make souls ready for heaven. At the last judgment, when the resurrection of the dead sees immortal soul joined with glorified body, purgatory is done away with: only heaven and hell will remain.

A reasonable, and commonsensical, theological question could be asked about Catholic understandings of the afterlife: why is an intermediate state before heaven necessary? After all, sins are either forgiven or they are not. But as simple as this query might seem, Catholic doctrine has maintained a complex economy of forgiveness, centering on the sacrament of penance. A sacrament, formally understood, is a rite that transmits grace, "an efficacious sign" that "dispenses divine life."[16] The sacrament of penance, now more commonly referred to as "the sacrament of reconciliation" or simply "confession," refers to confession and absolution of sin through the mediation of a priest. But along with confession and absolution, penance is necessary—penance being understood as a kind of self-punishment, reflecting both an internal and external need and desire to express sorrow and fulfill to the demands of justice. Nowadays, penance comes in the form of prayers said immediately after confession. In times past, however, penance was quite elaborate and would include acts like walking to church on one's knees or going on pilgrimage. And so, even though sins are forgiven, there is still a process of punishment or purification necessary for the vestiges of sin to be erased. For those who are insufficiently purified, purgatory is that place where they can be purged of the last remaining taint of sin. Then there are those who have committed lesser sins, called "venial sins," that do not prevent them from obtaining heaven but nonetheless are blemishes on the soul, which need to be wiped away. Purgatory provides just such an intermediate state in which our souls can be cleansed.

In sum, the traditional Catholic view of purgatory rests upon the assumption that God created human beings so they may enter heaven and God's presence for eternity. Hell exists for those who persist in their opposition to God in and through death. But there are those who neither are totally reconciled with God nor totally opposed to him at the time when their earthly life ends. These souls must be purified before they can enter the divine presence. A scriptural corollary to this belief in the necessity of purification can be found in Revelation 21:27, which states that nothing "impure" can enter heaven. Given this understanding, purgatory then is not so much a place as it is a process.

The development of purgatory as a doctrine is historically quite complex. Most Catholic commentators would admit that there is nothing explicitly about purgatory in scripture. Instead, it would be better to say that the doctrine of purgatory is an extrapolation from revelation and practices of the earliest Christians. Early Christians did indeed pray for the dead and masses were said for them.[17] Over time, theologians elaborated the implications of this belief. For example, Origen, a Christian philosopher writing in the third century AD, referred to 1 Corinthians chapter 3 when he envisioned a threefold trial by fire after death: the fire of judgment, through which the righteous pass before going straightaway heaven; the "fire of combustion," which those who have minor sins must endure; and an eternal period in cleansing flame, which inveterate sinners suffer.[18] As Jacques Le Goff observes, the concept of purgatory is considered by most scholars to assume a definable shape in the writings of Cyprian in the third century AD, which make reference to the purification of sins through suffering in fire.[19]

When purgatory was explicitly addressed in the Council of Florence in 1439, the image of purifying fire was avoided in favor of the concept of purifying pains—a concept that drew heavily on the pronouncements of the Second Council of Lyons, which was held over 150 years earlier in 1274.[20] Purgatory, as a place of purifying punishment, or purgation, was explicitly affirmed by the Council of Trent in its "Decree on Purgatory," promulgated in 1547, which reads, in part, as follows:

> Whereas the Catholic Church, instructed by the Holy Ghost, has, from the sacred writings and the ancient tradition of the Fathers, taught, in sacred councils, and very recently in this oecumenical Synod, that there is a Purgatory, and that the souls there detained are helped by the suffrages of the faithful, but principally by the acceptable sacrifice of the altar; the holy Synod enjoins on bishops that they diligently endeavour that the sound doctrine concerning Purgatory, transmitted by the holy Fathers and sacred councils, be believed, maintained, taught, and everywhere proclaimed by the faithful of Christ.[21]

Given the phrasing and its declaration within an ecumenical council, I would argue that purgatory has the status of a dogma: a divinely revealed truth, and thus with a place within the Sacred Magisterium.

This penitential understanding of purgatory, and its seemingly uncompromising perfectionism, gave rise to real and deep-seated concerns throughout Catholic religious life. When my father said to me that he would go to purgatory, he was speaking as many Catholics of the time would: after all, who among us can say that she or he is pure enough to enter the kingdom of heaven?

But there is hope, for the time in purgatory can be relieved by what is called an "indulgence." An indulgence, which can only be granted by the pope, is a full or partial release of punishment in purgatory for sins that have already been forgiven.[22] A famous and controversial example of such an indulgence was called the Sabbatine privilege. The Sabbatine privilege is a promise given to people who faithfully wear the scapular, a piece of brown cloth with an image of the Virgin Mary on it that has been specially blessed. In addition to wearing the scapular, a person must observe and comply with the following requirements in order to receive remission from purgatorial purification:

> Observe chastity according to their state of life
> Recite daily the Little Office of the Blessed Virgin Mary, or
> Abstain from meat on Wednesdays and Saturdays, or
> Accomplish faithfully some other similar sacrifice.[23]

Even more famously, the buying and selling of indulgences was one of the precipitating causes of the Protestant Reformation in the sixteenth century and was roundly condemned by Protestants such as Martin Luther and the authors of the Ten Conclusions of Berne. While indulgences can no longer be sold, the papal practice of giving indulgences does persist. For example, Pope Francis offered an indulgence for the Extraordinary Holy Year of Mercy, which concluded on 20 November 2016, that would have been gained by performing works of mercy as well as by meeting the standard conditions for receiving an indulgence, which include confessing one's sins.[24] Indulgences can also be transferred from the living to those souls in purgatory, and there is long tradition of purgatory cults in which Catholics perform penances and such so that the deceased can be released from purgatorial pains.[25]

Catholicism in the last half century has seen a number of substantial changes in its religious life and relationship to the world. The pivot for many of these changes was the Second Vatican Council, inaugurated by St. Pope John XXIII, in 1962. Purgatory was not given a great deal of attention in the Council's deliberations, and it has receded into the background of Catholic life: my father was educated as a kind of old-school Catholic and was very concerned about purgatory, but there is not the same level of focus or fear among Catholics nowadays.

But one does find renewed scholarly interest in purgatory under the rubric of what is called: *apokatastasis. Apokatastasis* is a Greek term that literally means "restitution" or "reconstitution" and refers to the universal salvific will of God and to the prospect that everyone, eventually, will be saved. The Catholic Church has always believed in hell. It also adheres to the proposition that outside of the Church there is no salvation: *Extra ecclesiam nullus salus.* But these propositions have been nuanced in countless ways, especially after the Second Vatican Council. For example, the Catholic Church most certainly teaches that non-Catholics and non-Christians can be saved. Within this framework, some theologians have speculated that essentially everyone will go through purgatory and thus have a chance of salvation. Some may indeed reject this opportunity, but in accord with the universal salvific will of God, we all can experience an *apokatastasis*, a reconstitution that will allow us to share the beatific vision in heaven.

IV. THE STATE OF LIMBO

Catholic teaching about purgatory belongs to the Sacred Magisterium, even though many Catholics do not mention it anymore and some might find the whole idea of purgatory unscriptural and archaic. The concept of limbo, by contrast, is more of a hypothesis that has belonged to the Ordinary Magisterium in its noninfallible iterations, which has now—for all intents and purposes—been abandoned.

The idea of limbo is intimately connected with traditional Catholic beliefs in baptism, particularly infant baptism. The Catholic understanding is that all human beings are born with original sin, which refers to an original imperfection that stems from Adam and Eve. It is baptism that cleanses us from original sin and, for that reason, the sacrament of baptism should be performed soon after a child is born.

I saw an example of this emphasis on infant baptism as I did research at a Catholic mission station in North India. While there, I looked at the mission station's baptismal records from the 1960s and found a large number of infant baptisms recorded. What I discovered was that these children who were brought to the mission's medical dispensary were sick and on the brink of death, and they were baptized so they could go to heaven. While this practice would now be considered highly unethical, it did represent a deep and pervasive Catholic emphasis on the importance of baptism and the fear that unbaptized children would be in a state of limbo.

Dante Alighieri drew his vision of limbo on the outskirts of hell from a catechism written by Honorius of Autun called the *Elucidarium*, which was used throughout the Middle Ages.[26] Honorius argued that the Saints of the Old Testament, along with unbaptized infants, would exist in limbo, which was described as a "place of darkness." Contemporaneously, the theologian Peter Abelard envisioned limbo as a place of punishment insofar as that the souls of those unbaptized infants are aware that they lack the beatific vision of heaven.[27] St. Thomas Aquinas, in his *Summa Theologica*, describes "children's limbo" as having "no pain of sense."[28] The trajectory of limbo as a theological hypothesis owes much to far earlier disputes between St. Augustine of Hippo and Pelagius and his supporters. In arguing strongly for the necessity of baptism for salvation, Augustine opened up a theological space for limbo by maintaining that unbaptized infants, while surely damned, will nonetheless undergo the softest conceivable punishment.[29] Augustine's position was described by George J. Dyer, in his survey *Limbo: Unsettled Question*, as marked by "vigor and vacillation."[30]

There was real tension between baptism being a necessary and indispensable ritual and the whole notion of God being merciful. After all, what sense can we make of a salvific economy that excludes infants who through no fault of their own were not baptized? So limbo remained a kind of hypothesis, a mediation between these two poles. It was mentioned in Catholic life and practice, but it was never defined doctrine and certainly never reached the level of a dogma.

In 2007, however, the International Theological Commission, which was begun by St. John Paul II, produced a statement that was approved by then Pope Benedict XVI: It reads as follows:

> Our conclusion is that the many factors that we have considered above give serious theological and liturgical grounds for hope that unbaptized infants who die will be saved and enjoy the beatific vision. We emphasize that these are reasons for prayerful hope, rather than grounds for sure knowledge. There is much that simply has not been revealed to us. We live by faith and hope in the God of mercy and love who has been revealed to us in Christ, and the Spirit moves us to pray in constant thankfulness and joy. . . . What has been revealed to us is that the ordinary way of salvation is by the sacrament of baptism. None of the above considerations should be taken as qualifying the necessity of baptism or justifying delay in administering the sacrament. Rather, as we want to reaffirm in

conclusion, they provide strong grounds for hope that God will save infants when we have not been able to do for them what we would have wished to do, namely, to baptize them into the faith and life of the Church.[31]

What this statement reveals is an ongoing Catholic doctrinal development concerning the nature of baptism. I think it would be fair to say that baptism is still crucial, but the necessity of performing the ritual itself is superseded by a more expansive understanding of a baptism of the heart or even an unconscious baptism. As a result, limbo has fallen away from serious discussion in most Catholic intellectual life.

V. LATTER-DAY SAINT AND CATHOLIC DISCUSSIONS

What the discarding of limbo as a hypothesis also reveals is that Catholic doctrinal thinking is evolving, or continues to evolve. While Catholic doctrine is often presented and understood as timeless truths that are reaffirmed through time, the fact of the matter is that Catholic doctrine has changed in a number of specific ways—such as its opinion regarding slavery and usury, for example—and even while many of those changes reflect changes in continuity with the central tenets of the Catholic faith, they do respond to changes in the context in which Catholics and all human beings live their lives.

This is especially the case in how heaven is described. I have used the formulation "beatific vision," which is the standard way of describing heaven in Catholic parlance. But the definition or understanding of what the beatific vision means has deepened. Classically, the beatific vision had been understood to mean the contemplation of God. More recently, however, some Catholic theologians have understood the beatific vision as a union with God—quite literally a *theosis*: not just becoming one with God but becoming God.

While this understanding of *theosis* is still different from what Latter-day Saints mean by exaltation, it does suggest that there is still much to talk about between Catholics and Latter-day Saints—as well as other Christians—about the life that awaits us beyond the grave. The status of body and matter itself are particularly suggestive areas where Latter-day Saints and Catholics can engage each other in thinking about the afterlife. For example, Catholic theologian Stephen Webb wrote insightfully on these questions before his untimely death and also authored a volume with Latter-day Saint scholar and Brigham Young University professor Alonzo L. Gaskill that serves as an exemplary model for Latter-day Saint and Roman Catholic dialogue.[32] But in addition to more abstract issues concerning the body and materiality, Christian discussions of the afterlife, across denominational boundaries, raise the most fundamental question: What do we have do to enter into God's presence after our earthly lives pass? What Latter-day Saints and Catholics do agree upon is that while the sacrificial death and atonement of Jesus Christ has opened up redemptive possibilities for all human beings, it is still necessary for all of us to exercise our own free will—our own agency—in order to draw near our Heavenly Father.

NOTES

1. For more on this practice and scene, see Mathew N. Schmalz, *Mercy Matters: Opening Yourself to the Life-Changing Gift* (Huntington, IN: Our Sunday Visitor Press, 2016).

2. For an example from the time of the Reformation that emphasizes how polemical these disputes can become, compare "The Ten Conclusions of Berne," a creedal statement written under the direction of Huldreich Zwingli and promulgated in 1528, with the "Creed of the Council of Trent," a key document of the Catholic "counter-reformation." Both can be found in John Leith, ed., *Creeds of the Churches: A Reader in Christian Doctrine from the Bible to the Present* (Louisville, KY: Westminster John Knox Press, 1982), 129–30, 440–42.

3. Dante Alighieri, *Purgatory*, trans. Rev. H. F. Carey, Project Guttenberg, 2014, https://www.gutenberg.org/files/8795/8795-h/8795-h.htm#link1.

4. For a pre-Vatican II survey of the development of purgatory and its status in Catholic doctrine, see *Catholic Encyclopedia*, s.v. "Purgatory," http://www .newadvent.org/cathen/12575a.htm.

5. Nick Pisa, "Pope Ends State of Limbo after 800 Years," *The Telegraph*, 23 April 2007, http://www.telegraph.co.uk/news/worldnews/1549439 /The-Pope-ends-state-of-limbo-after-800-years.html.

6. As indicated by the title, this article's focus is on Catholic views of purgatory and limbo. The faith's rich theology on the afterlife comprises other topics, including, for example, the doctrine of the resurrection. While a detailed discussion of the resurrection is outside the scope of this article, for additional details the reader may wish to consult other sources, such as the following: *United States Catholic Catechism for Adults* (Washington, DC: United Stakes Conference of Catholic Bishops, 2006), s.vv. "Resurrection of Jesus Christ" and "Resurrection of the Body"; Gerhard Lohfink, *Is This All There Is? On Resurrection and Eternal Life* (Collegeville, MN: Liturgical Press Academic, 2018); Pheme Perkins, *Resurrection: New Testament Witness and Contemporary Reflection* (New York: Doubleday, 1984); John R. Sachs, "Resurrection of the Body," in *The HarperCollins Encyclopedia of Catholicism*, ed. Richard E. McBrien (San Francisco, CA: Harper San Francisco, 1995), 1110–11; Pheme Perkins, "Resurrection of Christ," in McBrien, *HarperCollins Encyclopedia*, 1108–10; Stephen Davis, Daniel Kendall, and Gerald O'Collins, eds., *The Resurrection* (New York: Oxford University Press, 1998).

7. The formal way to refer to the Church, in Catholic parlance, is as "she" or "her."

8. "Catechism of the Catholic Church," La Santa Sede, 2003, http://www .vatican.va/archive/ccc_css/archive/catechism/p1s1c2a2.htm.

9. Avery Cardinal Dulles, *Magisterium: Teacher and Guardian of the Faith* (Naples, FL: Sapientia Press, 2007), 3.

10. Dulles, *Magisterium*, 77. See also "Congregation for the Doctrine of the Faith: Instruction: Donam Veritatis: On the Ecclesial Vocation of the Theologian," La Santa Sede, 1990, http://www.vatican.va/roman_curia/congregations /cfaith/documents/rc_con_cfaith_doc_19900524_theologian-vocation_ en.html.

11. For a helpful overview of the category "definitive teaching," see Ladislas Orsy, *Receiving the Council: Theological and Canonical Insights and Debates* (Collegeville, MN: Liturgical Press, 2009), 129–42.

12. For example, see Francis A. Sullivan, *Creative Fidelity: Weighing and Interpreting Documents of the Magisterium* (Eugene, OR: WIPF and Stock Publishers, 1996).

13. Hans Urs von Balthasar, *Dare We Hope That "All Men Be Saved?"* (San Francisco: Ignatius Books, 1988).

14. Karl Rahner, "Anonymous Christians," *Theological Investigations* (New York: Seabury Press, 1974), 6:390–91. See also Mathew N. Schmalz, "Transcendental Reduction: Karl Rahner's Theory of Anonymous Christianity. I," *Vidyajyoti Journal of Theological Reflection* 59 (October 1995): 680–92.

15. "Catechism of the Catholic Church," 1022.

16. "Catechism of the Catholic Church," 1131.

17. *Catholic Encyclopedia*, s.v. "Prayers for the Dead," http://www.newadvent.org/cathen/04653a.htm.

18. Jacques Le Goff, *The Birth of Purgatory* (Chicago: University of Chicago Press, 1984), 56.

19. Le Goff, *Birth of Purgatory*, 57.

20. Joseph Gill, *The Council of Florence* (Cambridge: Cambridge University Press, 2011), 120.

21. J. Waterworth, ed. and trans., "The Decree on Purgatory," *The Canons and Decrees of the Sacred and Oecumenical Council of Trent* (London: Dolman, 1848), 232–33.

22. United States Council of Catholic Bishops, *Manual of Indulgences* (Washington, DC: USCCB, 2006), 13.

23. Remi Amelunxen, "The Sabbatine Privilege and the 30 Gregorian Masses," Tradition in Action, http://www.traditioninaction.org/religious/d026_Sabbatine.htm; see also Rev. Eamon R. Carroll, O. Carm., "An Explanation of the Sabbatine Privilege," Order of Carmelites, http://www.ocarm.org/en/content/ocarm/explanation-sabbatine-privilege.

24. Pope Francis, *Misericordiae Vultus* (New York: Pauline Books & Media, 2015).

25. For a discussion of purgatory cults that draws upon a psychoanalytic method, see Michael Carroll, *Veiled Threats: The Logic of Popular Catholicism in Italy* (Baltimore and London: Johns Hopkins University Press, 1996).

26. George J. Dyer, *Limbo: Unsettled Question* (New York: Sheed & Ward, 1964), 5.

27. Peter Abelard, *Peter Abelard: Collationes*, ed. and trans. by John Marenbon and Giovanni Orlandi (Oxford: Clarendon Press, 2001), 126. For a

discussion more attuned to a broader audience, see Charles Penati, *Sacred Origins of Profound Things: The Stories Behind the Rites and Rituals of the World's Religions* (New York: Penguin Books, 1996), 490.

28. Thomas Aquinas, *Summa Theologica*, vol. 2, trans. Fathers of the English Dominican Province (Notre Dame, IN: 1948), Q89, art. 6, parts i–ii.

29. Augustine of Hippo, *The Augustine Catechism: The Enchiridion on Faith, Hope, and Charity*, trans. Bruce Harbart, ed. Boniface Ramsey (Hyde Park, NY: New City Press, 2008), 20.

30. Dyer, *Limbo: Unsettled Question*, 15.

31. "International Theological Commission: The Hope of Salvation for Infants Who Die Without Being Baptised," La Santa Sede, 2007, http://www .vatican.va/roman_curia/congregations/cfaith/cti_documents/rc_con _cfaith_doc_20070419_un-baptised-infants_en.html.

32. Stephen Webb, *Jesus Christ, Eternal God: Heavenly Flesh and the Metaphysics of Matter* (Oxford: Oxford University Press, 2011); Stephen H. Webb, *Mormon Christianity: What Other Christians Can Learn from Latter-day Saints* (Oxford: Oxford University Press, 2013); Stephen H. Webb and Alonzo L. Gaskill, *Catholic and Mormon: A Theological Conversation* (Oxford: Oxford University Press, 2015); see also Mathew N. Schmalz, "In Memoriam: Stephen Webb," *Dialogue: A Journal of Mormon Thought* 49, no. 3 (Fall 2016): 199–210.

Chapter 2

CHANGED BY GRACE

SOME INTRODUCTORY THOUGHTS ON THE EASTERN ORTHODOX UNDERSTANDING OF DEATH AND THE AFTERLIFE

Metropolitan Nikitas

His Eminence Metropolitan Nikitas of the Dardanelles (Lulias) is an Eastern Orthodox scholar and director of the Patriarch Athenagoras Orthodox Institute in Berkeley, California.

Throughout history, humanity has struggled to come to terms with death and issues surrounding the afterlife. To answer the questions of the faithful and help guide them on their spiritual quest and journey, religious teachers offered instruction on these matters. Through the centuries and with the influence of various contributing factors, doctrinal teachings about death and the afterlife were formulated. These teachings often came as a response or clarification to the questions which challenged the believer. It was in this style and manner that the theological positions of the Eastern Orthodox Church on death and the afterlife developed. In some cases, it may be safe to say that the Orthodox Church is still developing her theological statements on certain positions, as humanity faces new challenges and issues in this field.

Although many of the theological foundations had been set in the Hebrew scriptures, the teachings and resurrection of Jesus brought new meaning and implications. This is clear and evident in the writings of St. Paul, who says:

> But we would not have you ignorant, brethren, concerning those who are asleep, that you may not grieve as others do who have no hope.
>
> For since we believe that Jesus died and rose again, even so, through Jesus, God will bring with him those who have fallen asleep.
>
> For this we declare to you by the word of the Lord, that we who are alive, who are left until the coming of the Lord shall not precede those who have fallen asleep.
>
> For the Lord himself will descend from heaven with a cry of command, with the archangel's call, and with the sound of the trumpet of God. And the dead in Christ will rise first;
>
> Then we who are alive, who are left, shall be caught up together with them in the clouds to meet the Lord in the air; and so we shall always be with the Lord.[1]

The words of Paul, though, did not provide all the answers; questions and confusion remained. Later authors would contribute to the process of defining and refining the doctrines concerning death and the afterlife.

The themes of death, resurrection, and the afterlife are the very heart and core of the Eastern Orthodox Christian faith. These teachings are affirmed not only in the Nicaean Creed, which is recited at every Divine Liturgy and many other liturgical services, but also beautifully expressed in the prayers read by the clergy during the celebration of the Liturgy of Saint Basil. "He brought us to the knowledge of You, the true God and Father, redeeming us to Himself as a chosen race, a royal priesthood, a holy nation, and, when He had cleansed us in water and sanctified us with the Holy Spirit, He gave Himself up as a ransom to death, to which we were in bondage, sold under sin. He descended into Hades by way of the Cross, that He might fill all things in Himself and loosed the pangs of death. Rising on the third day, He prepared the way for the resurrection of all flesh from the dead, because it was not possible for Him (the Author of life) to be held by it."[2]

While many people see death as the end of the life cycle, the Orthodox Christian understands that it is only a step into the next phase of life, the resurrection of all as mentioned in the Gospel of John. For the believer, death is not an end in itself; rather, it is a necessary passageway into eternity. Still, death has always been and remains a mystery, incomprehensible to human intellect and reason.

A noted Orthodox author writes the following: "From the time death entered into the world as a consequence of sin, no one has looked upon death with indifference. And while we all accept that death is the estate of life, we find it impossible to imagine ourselves dead! But whether we comprehend this or not, from the moment we come into this world, we are indeed destined to die. Furthermore, while death comes only once in our lifetime, we fear it every day. And death is inexorable. It comes as a skeleton holding a large sickle—to 'reap' man, not allowing him to take anything with him. And when one of our fellow human beings crosses over to the opposite side, the rest of us remain on this side frightened and bewildered."[3]

In order to understand the teachings of the Eastern Orthodox tradition concerning death and the afterlife, one must start at the very beginning. One must reflect on creation itself. A hymn by Saint John of Damascus, the noted theologian and hymnographer, states: "When in Your image and likeness You in the beginning did create and fashion man You gave him a home in Paradise, and made him the chief of your creation. But by the devil's envy, alas, beguiled to eat the fruit forbidden, transgressor then of your commandments he became; wherefore back to earth, from which he was first taken, you did sentence him to return again, O Lord, and to pray you to give him rest."[4] Death, then, comes as a result of the transgression and disobedience of the first created, Adam and Eve, who failed to reach their true calling. Because of their action of disobedience, they and the created world are in a state of "fallen nature." This state allows not only for corruption and decay but also for death.

But God did not create the human race to have death as an end; rather, he created humanity to enter into communion with him into eternity.

As part of the plan of divine economy, God's plan for the restoration of creation, "when the time had fully come, God sent forth his Son, born of woman, born under the law, to redeem those who were under the law, so that we might receive adoption as sons."[5] Christ came into the world to save and redeem fallen humanity and restore the fallen world to a natural state. Saint Romanos the Melodist puts this theological matter into poetic words in one of the stanzas found in the Akathist Hymn. He writes: "Wishing to save the world, the Creator of all came to us of His own will. Being at once our Shepherd and our God, He appeared among us as a man. And, appearing as we are, He called us to Himself."[6] Through his word and teachings, Christ offered the path that would lead the believer back to the kingdom, including passing from death into life. With these thoughts in mind, one can understand that death was no longer understood as a curse. Rather, the love of God was able to transform death into a blessing and this gave the means for humanity to resume its true journey to union with God.

For the Orthodox Christian, death is understood as a means of passage, as it is the moment when the soul leaves the body and travels to the place where it shall remain until the general resurrection. This act of separation is described by Saint John of Damascus in the hymns of the funeral services, where he writes, "Indeed, how awesome is the mystery of our death! How the soul is forcibly severed from its harmonious union with the body, and this natural bond of coexistence is broken by divine will."[7] The theology of the Fall, death, and the separation of soul and body are expressed in the great prayer of forgiveness which a hierarch reads at the end of the funeral service. The prayer goes as follows: "O Lord our God, in your inexpressible wisdom you created man out of the earth, giving him form and adorning him with beauty, as a precious and heavenly being, to the praise and honor of your glory and kingdom, making him in your image and likeness. But when he violated your commandment and did not preserve the image which had been entrusted to him, so that this evil state should not endure forever, in your love for mankind you ordered that this mixture and blend, and the unbroken bond that you established, O God of our Fathers, should by your will be severed and dissolved; and that the soul should proceed until the general resurrection to the place from where it received its being, and that the body should be dissolved into the elements from which it was made."[8]

It is clear and evident in both the hymn and the prayer that at death, the soul and body separate. Even those who do not believe in God understand that the "life force" leaves the human body and one is, then, dead. For the Orthodox Christian, though, it is not such an easy or simple formula. At death, the body begins the process of returning to the elements of which it was made, while the soul awaits the time of the great and glorious general resurrection when all shall rise from the tombs. The soul continues to have its own existence after its separation from the body. This is affirmed by the words of Jesus in the Gospel of Matthew when he says, "And do not fear those who kill the body but cannot kill the soul."[9] These thoughts and statements leave questions which need to be answered, especially the question of "where does the soul reside after death?" Saint John Chrysostom responds to this question in his homilies on the Gospel of Matthew. He tells his audience that the souls go to "a place" and there they wait for the universal resurrection.[10] While there are no details as to "the place," it would be best to understand it as a spiritual realm and not "a place" as defined by space and other human expressions.

It would be proper, at this point, to make a few comments related to the body following the death of a person. It is important to understand that in the Eastern Orthodox tradition, special attention and care are given to the body of the deceased, "as the body is a temple of the Holy Spirit," as Paul states in the letter to the Christian community in Corinth.[11] In some places, there are special rites for washing and preparation of the body, which are a reflection of the anointing and preparation of the body of Christ. A type of burial shroud is even used in some parts of the Orthodox world, again reminding one of Christ and his own burial. In the strictest expression of Eastern Orthodoxy, the body is not to be cremated or given to science for research. These actions are understood by many to be a type of irreverence shown for God's creation and such practices would be seen as harmful and destructive. In fact, in traditional Orthodox lands there is no embalming, so the body may return to the earth as soon as possible. The embalming of a person would only serve as an obstacle in the natural process. The faithful are reminded of this when the clergy recite the following words when pouring some earth on the body of the dead person: "The earth is the Lord's and the fullness thereof the world and those who dwell therein; you are earth and to earth you shall return."[12] Of course, in the United States and in many other lands where family members may need extra time to travel to the funeral, embalming has become the natural and customary practice in most Christian communities. While this practice may seem good and necessary, it distorts the natural process that the hymns and prayers of the Orthodox funeral service imply. Clearly, the body is to return to the place of its origin, the earth. This matter becomes quite challenging in places where cremation is mandatory. Or what of those who have died in a fire and were never properly buried? These and other similar questions are the exception to the rule and not the standard measure.

Christians, according to the Eastern Orthodox expression of faith, do not focus on death. Rather, the focus and central theological doctrine rests on the crucifixion and the resurrection of Jesus, who rose from the dead in his glorified body. The two are inseparable. Through and with the resurrection of Christ, a new time and age begin. The pages of old are closed and new chapters are to be written. Death no longer has power and authority, as it has been conquered by Jesus. In this way, one understands that Christ opened for all humanity the way to incorruptibility—to immortality and eternal life.

At some point in time, all things shall come to pass and there will be a final judgment. In *The Evergetinos*, a compilation of sayings and teachings of Church Fathers and monastics, one reads the following concerning the Final Judgment:

The Lord says in the Gospel: "Walk while ye have the light" (St. John 12:35). Also, through the Prophet He says: "In an acceptable time have I heard thee, and in a day of salvation have I helped thee" (Isaiah 49:8). This saying of the Prophet is interpreted by the Apostle, who says: "Behold, now is the accepted time; behold, now is the day of salvation" (II Corinthians 6:2). And a similar thought is expressed by the wise Solomon, when he says: "Whatsoever thy hands findeth to do, do it with thy might, for there is no work, nor device, nor knowledge, nor wisdom in the grave, whither thou goest" (Ecclesiastes 9:10). From all of these Biblical testimonies, it is clearly demonstrated that in the moral state in which one departs from this world, in the same state will he appear before the impartial Judgment Seat, in order to be judged.[13]

Orthodox Christians believe that until that moment in time, those who have left this life will experience a foretaste of the kingdom. Once the final judgment is passed, the righteous, though, will enjoy the blessings that have been prepared for them "from the foundation of the world."[14] The sinners and those who have failed in their true calling will also journey to their respective place for eternity. The Fathers of the Church have expressed their thoughts on this matter and have put into words what is to be expected. In the patristic tradition regarding the righteous, one finds expressions that call eternal life "the real life." The hymnography and prayers of the Church speak of the blessed state and place as being "without pain, without sorrow, a place where there is no mourning."[15] Saint Basil the Great writes: "That land is of the living where night does not exist and where there is no sleep, the imitation of death. There, there is no material eating and drinking—the supports of our weakness; there are no sicknesses, no pains, no medicines, no courts of law, no businesses, no crafts, and no money—the beginning of evils, the subject of wars, and the root of enmity. It is the land of the living, not of the dying because of sin, but of the living the true life in Christ Jesus."[16]

The placement of a person in the kingdom of God is the return and restoration of humanity to full communion with God, which is the purpose and ultimate calling of humanity. In Orthodox theological language, the term *theosis* is often translated as "deification." It is what is stated in 2 Peter 1:4 when he writes that we are to "become partakers of divine nature." Human nature is not obliterated and lost; rather, it is transformed and changed by grace. It is impossible, though, to fully comprehend what this means, as it is beyond all human understanding and logic. Metropolitan Kallistos Ware writes the following, which might offer a better understanding of the theological implication this carries, "The aim of the Christian life, which Seraphim described as the acquisition of the Holy Spirit of God, can equally well be defined in terms of deification. Basil described the human person as a creature who has received the order to become a god; and Athanasius, as we know, said that God became human that we humans might become god. 'In My kingdom, said Christ, I shall be God with you as gods.' Such, according to the teaching of the Orthodox Church, is the final goal at which every Christian must aim: to become god, to attain *theosis*, 'deification' or 'divinization'. For Orthodoxy our salvation and redemption means our deification."[17]

In the text *Learning Theology with the Church Fathers*, Christopher Hall draws from the ancient tradition of the Church and brings to the attention of the reader various materials from the Fathers. In his chapter on the resurrection of the body, he quotes Saint Justin the Martyr, who says: "Christ has come in his power from the almighty Father, . . . calling all men to friendship, benediction, repentance and community, which should take place in the same land of all the saints (Canaan), of which he has pledged that there shall be an allotted portion for all the faithful. . . . Wherefore, men from every land, whether slaves or free men, who believe in Christ and recognize the truth of his words and those of the Prophets, fully realize that they will one day be united with him in that and, to inherit imperishable blessings for all eternity."[18]

These thoughts can be understood when one looks at an Orthodox icon of the last judgment. In the center of the icon, Christ sits upon the throne and judges the nations. Surrounding him are the Theotokos, the Saints, and those who have been found just and righteous, according to his standards and measures. They shine in the glory of the light which comes from him. They stand and radiate in the warmth of his illuminating glory. These are the persons who have heard the calling, followed the path, and entered through the narrow gate. These are the sheep in the parable of the Last Judgment. The sinners and those not found worthy of his kingdom, though, burn and are consumed in the fire. These are those who have failed in the journey of life and those who have rejected the invitation to the eternal banquet of life; they are the goats spoken of in the parable. For the sinners, the light consumes and burns; for the righteous, the light illumines and glorifies. They sit in the company of Christ and enjoy that blessing that was promised to them.

The above thoughts and statements only open the door for exploration and study, as the theology and teachings concerning death and the afterlife are rather complex. May these words entice the reader to study further and explore the depth of Orthodox beauty.

NOTES

1. 1 Thessalonians 4:13–17. This passage is used in the Orthodox funeral service. All scripture quotes are from the Revised Standard Version.
2. St. Basil the Great, *Liturgy of St. Basil*, trans. Leonidas Contos and Spencer Kezios (Narthex Press, 2007), 22.
3. Nikolaos P. Vassiliadis, *The Mystery of Death* (Athens, Greece: The Orthodox Brotherhood of Theologians, 1993), 3.
4. Orthodox funeral service, Idiomela of St. John of Damascus, Grave Tone. All liturgical translations are the author's own, based on the Greek text in Evagoras Constantinidis, ed., *The Priest's Service Book (Mikron Euchologion, Agiasmatarion)* (Merrilville, IN: Father Evagoras Constantinides, 1989), 223.
5. Galatians 4:4–5.
6. Spencer Kezios, trans., *The Akathist Hymn* (Narthex Press, 2008), 98.

7. Orthodox funeral service, Idiomela of St. John of Damascus, fourth tone. See Constantinidis, *The Priest's Service Book (Mikron Euchologion, Agiasmatarion)*, 220.

8. Constantinidis, *Priest's Service Book*, 233.

9. Matthew 10:28.

10. See J.-P. Migne, *Patrologiae: Series Graeca* (Paris: Migne, 1857), 57:353–54.

11. See 1 Corinthians 6:19.

12. Orthodox funeral service, final anointing of the deceased before the casket is sealed. See Constantinidis, *Priest's Service Book*, 237.

13. Hrmk. Patapios, ed., *Evergetinos: Sayings of the Desert Fathers* (Center for Traditionalist Orthodox Studies, 2008), 4:357.

14. Matthew 25:34.

15. Orthodox funeral service, Kontakion. See Constantinidis, *Priest's Service Book*, 218.

16. St. Basil the Great, *On Psalm 104:5*, in Migne, *Patrologiae: Series Graeca*, 29:493.

17. Timothy Ware, *The Orthodox Church: An Introduction to Eastern Christianity*, 3rd rev. ed. (London: Penguin Books, 2015), 225.

18. Justin Martyr, *Dialogue with Trypho*, 139, in Christopher A. Hall, *Learning Theology with the Church Fathers* (Downers Grove, IL: IVP Academic, 2002), 254.

Chapter 3

THE DEAD ARE RAISED— BUT HOW AND WHY?

CONVERSATIONS WITH THE CHURCH'S FATHERS AND MOTHERS OF THE FIRST FIVE CENTURIES

Dennis Okholm

Dennis Okholm, an Anglican scholar, is a professor of theology at Azusa Pacific University.

"Even though fire destroy all traces of my flesh, the world receives the vaporized matter; and though dispersed through rivers and seas, or torn in pieces by wild beasts, I am laid up in the storehouses of a wealthy Lord. And, although the poor and the godless know not what is stored up, yet God the Sovereign, when He pleases, will restore the substance that is visible to Him alone to its pristine condition." —Tatian, *To the Greeks*

Among the first five centuries of the Christian church, theologians' explanations of death, resurrection, and—as N. T. Wright puts it—life after life after death, are not monolithic, though there are common threads and themes that wend their way through these centuries. And though emphases and themes varied from time to time (such as less attention to millennial expectations as history moved farther from New Testament predictions), the list of questions which begged for answers was perennial. Augustine's recitation in the *Concerning the City of God against the Pagans*[1] nicely summarizes the questions that preoccupied the preceding theological discussions, the most difficult of which was "When someone's body has been eaten by another man, who turns to cannibalism on the compulsion of hunger, into whose body will it return?" Augustine made the answer more difficult by arguing, contrary to what some had insisted upon, that what is consumed does not simply pass through the body but is ingested to supply nutrients to the consumer.

Though cannibalism might not be at the forefront of *our* questions about death, resurrection, and what lies beyond, what is called "chain consumption" might be something about which we might wonder, and certainly most of the other concerns discussed in the early centuries are precisely those of thoughtful Christians today.

So, even though there is not always unanimity of agreement in the answers, it would be instructive to enter into a conversation with several of these early church fathers—or mothers, in the case of Gregory's sister Macrina[2]—as if they were our contemporaries, a conversation about a range of topics that have to do with the resurrection of the body.

Though the nature of the resurrected body was often disputed in the early church,[3] the affirmation of bodily resurrection was as strong as the Apostle Paul's insistence in 1 Corinthians 15 of Christ's resurrection. The apologist Justin asked, "Why did He rise in the flesh in which He suffered, unless to show the resurrection of the flesh?"[4] He then records Gospel accounts of Christ proving his resurrected flesh to the disciples, and that it was not impossible for flesh to "ascend into heaven." Justin's reprimand for unbelief follows: "If, therefore, after all that has been said, any one demand demonstration of the resurrection, he is in no respect different from the Sadducees, since the resurrection of the flesh is the power of God, and, being above all reasoning, is established by faith, and seen in works."[5] A few decades earlier, Ignatius had pointed out that those who pierced Christ would not be able to see the one they had pierced and that they would "mourn for themselves" if Christ returned without a body.[6]

Besides answering objections such as those who say the salvation of the flesh is disadvantageous because it is the cause of our sins and infirmities, as well those who say that the flesh is imperfect if it does not rise with all its parts, Justin joins others who were out to refute the heresy of Docetism: "maintain[ing] that even Jesus Himself appeared only as spiritual, and not in flesh, but presented merely the appearance of flesh."[7] Tertullian will be even more adamant, accusing those who deny the resurrection of repudiating the flesh's creator *and* denying or changing the flesh's existence in Christ, "corrupting the very Word of God Himself, who became flesh, either by mutilating or misinterpreting the Scripture, and introducing, above all, apocryphal mysteries *and* blasphemous fables."[8]

But it is not merely the example of Christ's incarnate flesh and resurrected body that ensures the believer's bodily resurrection. As Tertullian makes clear, it is also Christ's present mediatorial role in his incarnate nature at the right hand of the Father that guarantees our future resurrection: "He keeps in his own self the deposit of the flesh which has been committed to him by both parties—the pledge and security of its entire perfection. For as "He has given to us the earnest of the Spirit," so has He received from us the earnest of the flesh, and has carried it with him into heaven as a pledge of that complete entirety which is one day to be restored to it."[9]

That God has sufficient power to raise dead bodies is, as Athenagoras puts it, "shown by the creation of these same bodies."[10] And the pledge of our everlasting continuance is based on God's purpose in creating humans, which was *not* to fill any need of or usefulness for the Creator, but to make an intelligent creature who could become a spectator of God's grandeur and "of the wisdom that is manifest in all things"—the contemplation of which God desires that humans always continue.[11]

Justin joins the chorus and insists that God would no more neglect his work and allow it to be annihilated than would a sculptor or painter, nor is it beneath this divine artist to raise flesh made of earth and "full of wickedness" since God created humans in his own image from dirt in the first place (Genesis 1:26).[12] Indeed, argued Irenaeus, if God does not raise the dead, then God lacks power; if God cannot impart life to bodies, then God's power and benevolence are restrained by something more powerful.[13] Augustine later insists that this applies even to bodies that have been consumed by wild beasts, burned up by fire, disintegrated into dust and ashes, dissolved in liquid, or evaporated into the air; nothing can "elude the notice or evade the power of the Creator of all things."[14]

Of course, our conversation partners tell us that we should not be surprised at the Creator's ability, since there is evidence of resurrection everywhere we look in God's handiwork. They point to the cycle of seasons, the night that turns to day, trees that produce fruit, the waxing and waning of the moon, recovery from illness, awakening from sleep, and the generation of humans "from a little drop of moisture."[15]

And then there is the seed metaphor, which Caroline Walker Bynum says is emphasized out of proportion to its use in the early church, but which is indeed prevalent in the conversation as Paul's analogy from 1 Corinthians 15:36–45 is reiterated many times.[16] And what is most significant about it is that the analogy—moving from the *dissolution* of what is sown to the plant that springs up—raises questions about continuity, identity, and integrity that occupy a good share of the discussion of resurrection. Gregory of Nyssa, for example, used the seed metaphor to illustrate how resurrection worked. He explained that just as a seed grows into a plant, so when we are resurrected we will not be the same, but not entirely different either. We will have "great and splendid additions."[17] This comment, however, generates some concerns as well.

He seems to recognize the issues this raises because he finds a similarity to the resurrected human in the seed that leaves behind some of its aspects while not leaving and losing itself; in the same way, he says: "The human being deposits in death all those peculiar surroundings which it has acquired from passionate propensities; dishonor, I mean, in corruption and weakness and characteristics of age; and yet the human being does not lose itself. It changes into an ear of corn as it were; into incorruption, that is, and glory and honor and power and absolute perfection; into a condition in which its life is no longer carried on in the ways peculiar to mere nature, but has passed into a spiritual and passionless existence." Of course, Gregory was by no means the first to admit that the resurrected body is different than what preceded it. The second-century apologist Athenagoras had recognized that the resurrection is "a species of change, and the last of all, and a change for the better of what still remains in existence at that time," especially since what is resurrected to immortality is a mortal body, the continuation of which was interrupted by "the dissolution of its parts."[18]

What Gregory, Athenagoras, and a host of others were aware of are the difficulties that a Christian doctrine of bodily resurrection entails. If what is sown is a biodegradable body and what is raised is a body that is incorruptible and immortal, how is that the same body? In fact, since our bodies are always changing from conception to death, which "body" is raised? And if we suffer amputations, inequalities, deformities, or deficiencies, are those retained in the resurrected body, and, if not, again, how is the resurrected body the same as that body? And, then, there is Augustine's "most difficult" question about "chain consumption" or cannibalism, which raises the more general concern about the scattered parts of a human body that must somehow be reassembled into the original at the resurrection. In the end, the issue is really about identity, especially for Christians who disavow the transmigration of souls.[19] Or, to put it in the words of the Apostle Paul, "How are the dead raised? With what kind of body will they come?" (1 Corinthians 15:35) The early theologians were preoccupied with this question. Bynum even admits that the "basic conclusion" of her study of resurrection in the first fourteen centuries of the Western church is that "a concern for material and structural continuity showed remarkable persistence even where it seemed almost to require philosophical incoherence, theological equivocation, or aesthetic offensiveness."[20] However, Bynum also points out that, though continuity was the issue, *identity* was not yet an *explicit* issue in the late first and early second centuries: "Neither in philosophical argument nor in image is the question yet raised: What would account for the 'me-ness' of the 'me' that returns?")[21]

These theologians were agreed that if the body that is raised is not the very same that died, then that individual who had died did not rise again.[22] Still, Gregory wonders about earthly bodies that are wracked by old age, disease, injuries, or death in infancy. He agrees with everyone else, but it leaves him with a question: "It comes then to this: that, if our bodies are to live again in every respect the same as before, this thing that we are expecting is simply a calamity; whereas if they are not the same, the person raised up will be another than he who died. . . . How, then, will the Resurrection affect myself, when instead of me some one else will come to life?" An adult is raised who died as a baby, a vibrant young man is raised who died an aged old man, and so on. And then Gregory states succinctly and poignantly:

> For who has not heard that human life is like a stream, moving from birth to death at a certain rate of progress, and then only ceasing from the progressive movement when it ceases also to exist? This movement indeed is not one of special change; our bulk never exceeds itself; but it makes this advance by means of internal alteration; and as long as this alteration is that which its name implies, it never remains at the same stage from moment to moment; for how can that which is being altered be kept in any sameness? . . . Just, then, as it is impossible for one who has touched that flame twice on the same place, to touch twice the very same flame, a thing of the same kind is found to be the case with the constitution of our body. . . . Then, a particular man is not the same even as he was yesterday, but is made different by this transmutation, when so be that the Resurrection shall restore our body to life again, that single man will become a crowd of human beings, so that with his rising again there will be found the babe, the child, the boy, the youth, the man, the father, the old man and all the intermediate persons that he once was.[23]

To further complicate matters, Gregory asks about those who have been both chaste and promiscuous, who have been both tortured for their faith and shrunk from it, or who first sin and then are cleansed by repentance and then relapse into sin again: "Which body, then, is the profligate to be tortured in? In that which is stiffened with old age and is near to death? But this is not the same as that which did the sin. In that, then, which defiled itself by giving way to passion? But where is the old man, in that case? This last, in fact, will not rise again, and the Resurrection will not do a complete work; or else he will rise, while the criminal will escape."[24]

What is bothering Gregory and others is how we can speak of change *and* identity. And it doesn't help that Gregory says at one point that "if the same man is to return into himself, he must be the same entirely, and regain his original formation in every single atom of his elements."[25] And those atoms must be composed around the same soul; otherwise, atoms mingle indiscriminately "with no distinct natural order," resulting in a blend and confusion that permits no distinctions of one thing from another. Humorously, if that be the case, Gregory says a man might gather flowers, hunt birds, or see humanity in hemlock or cut down corn but is really doing violence to fellow countrymen.[26]

So, to avoid such confusion, how do the "atoms" of a person who dies find each other, as it were, and come together at the resurrection? We can find a typical response if we turn to the East and the West.

Turning to the former, at one point Gregory of Nyssa speaks of the soul as if it were that which provides the stability for the constituent parts of the body that are in constant flux and change. The "form" that remains in the soul is a seal that impresses itself like a stamp on that which grows and diminishes and changes, so that what corresponded to the soul in the beginning, stamped by the form, properly belongs to the individual and will return to it "from the common source." The soul is "disposed to cling to and long for the body that has been wedded to it"—such "a close relationship and power of recognition" that dispersed atoms stream back together from wherever nature has arranged them when the signal is given by God, so that "following this force of the soul which acts upon the various atoms, all these, once so familiar with each other, rush simultaneously together and form the cable of the body by means of the soul, each single one of them being wedded to its former neighbor and embracing an old acquaintance." Gregory finds examples of this in mercury, in the plant that comes from the seed, and in the way an artist can reproduce a blend of dyes the same as before.[27]

Turning to the West, Augustine is not as elaborate as Gregory, but he can sound much like Gregory when, in his catechism, he assures his readers that "the earthly matter out of which the flesh of mortal man is created does not perish" and that regardless of what has happened to it—even if it has become food for beasts or even changed into the flesh of a cannibal—"in an instant it returns to that soul which first animated it so as to make it become a human being and to make it live and grow."[28] In a similar vein, he speaks of a "design implanted in the body of each person" or "a kind of pattern already imposed potentially on the material substance of the individual . . . like the pattern on a loom" or like the potentiality that is latent in a seed. He speculates that in the resurrection the body will be what it would be if it had attained maturity, though Augustine will not take issue with anyone who insists that every person is raised with "the precise stature he had when he departed this life," as long as it does not result in any ugliness, weakness, sluggishness, corruption, or anything else inconsistent with God's realm.[29]

What is implied in this final comment is that even if we speak of atoms coming home to roost, it may not be the case that all of them come home or, even if all do, that they come home reassembled as they once were. Indeed, Augustine does not take the biblical promise that "not a hair will perish" to mean that all nail and hair clippings will be preserved—especially if they all ended up producing deformity. He uses the analogy of an artist—a sculptor or a potter—to suggest that when the resurrection occurs, "those elements which disintegrated and were changed into this or that shape and form of other things" do return to the same body from which they were separated, but not necessarily to the very same body parts to which they originally belonged. Like the statue that is melted down or crushed to powder and like the pot that is reduced to a lump, *all* the material can be used to reconfigure a new statue or a new pot. Hairs need not return to hairs nor nails, to nails. But nothing will perish that is essential to the nature of a particular body, and anything in it that was deformed will be restored "in such a way as to remove the deformity while preserving the substance intact," for "in his Providence the Artist sees to it that nothing unseemly results."[30]

Likewise, the divine artist will also ensure that what is reconfigured is beautiful and harmonious with no deficiencies: "What was not yet complete would be made whole, just as what has been marred will be restored."[31] What about miscarriages, undeveloped fetuses, or births that are considered monstrosities due to the wrong number of appendages or missing body parts? Augustine argues that they "will at the resurrection be restored to the normal human shape." Even in the case of conjoined twins each will have its own body whole.[32] And, using the seed analogy again, Augustine says that even little children who die will instantly rise again not with tiny bodies but with the maturity they would have attained over time, for we have been conceived and born with what he calls a "limit of perfection"—a potentiality latent in the seed.[33]

Will there be inequalities in the resurrection life as there are in the present life? Ror instance, will the thin be thin and the fat, fat? Not necessarily, though God who created ex nihilo will preserve individuality and recognizable likeness, and even if there will be a "well-devised inequality," nothing will be "unseemly," for, says Augustine, physical beauty depends on harmony between the parts of the body.[34] The bodies of the saints will be raised free from any defect, deformity, corruption, encumbrance, or hindrance: "their freedom of action will be as complete as their happiness" with "the spirit quickening the subordinated flesh," and this is what is meant by "spiritual" bodies—but bodies nonetheless, of the same substance as the flesh of Jesus Christ even after his resurrection.[35] In a nutshell, Augustine says, "Thus there will be no ugliness, which is caused by such disharmony, when distortions have been corrected and unpleasing deficiencies supplied from resources known to the Creator, and unprepossessing excesses reduced without loss of essential substance."[36]

We should mention two caveats before considering the issue Augustine considered the most difficult. First, Augustine does say at one point that, though all human bodies will rise again with a body of the same size as they had or would have had in the prime of life, if it *is* the same kind of body (infant or old) one had when he or she died, no weakness will remain in body or mind.[37] Second, note that what was said in the previous paragraph Augustine said was true of "saints," for at one point he says that we should not care what happens to those who will be eternally damned with regard to whether their physical defects and deformities will continue or not.[38]

And now, what about those whose bodies have been consumed by animals or, worse, who have been eaten by cannibals (such as occurs among the "Greeks and barbarians")? This issue of "chain consumption" was addressed often by these early church apologists and theologians. Among them, Athenagoras discusses this at length and several times in his treatise on the resurrection. He argues that God has the power and skill "to separate that which has been broken up and distributed among a multitude of animals of all kinds" and "unite it again with the proper numbers and parts of members." True, he says, some parts of bodies are vomited or defecated, but even if what is digested gets changed into some aspect of the consuming body, it does not matter, "For the bodies that rise again are reconstituted from the parts which properly belong to them, whereas no one of the things mentioned is such a part, nor has it the form or place of a part; nay, it does not remain always with the parts of the body which are nourished, or rise again with the parts that rise, since no longer does blood, or phlegm, or bile, or breath, contribute anything to the life."[39] In other words, for Athenagoras the resurrected body is different from the present body. He assumes that it is against nature for like to consume like, so that even if a human consumes another human, the parts would not "stick": Athenagoras states that no matter what has happened to the body, whether "burnt up by fire, or rotted by water, or consumed by wild beasts," it will be able to successfully reunite itself at resurrection.[40]

Much of what we have dealt with above has to do with the attempts to ensure that the body that is raised is somehow constituted by the very same body that died. Yet, we *have* noted from time to time an admission that the body does change, even in this life, let alone with it transitions from mortality to immortality. These early Christians sometimes struggled to explain how that which changes could be the same.[41] How can that which in Pauline idiom is "sown a different body" be the same body as that which is resurrected? Again, to some extent we are harking back to the seed analogy in 1 Corinthians 15.

Early on, Tertullian handled this well by arguing that the resurrected body is not a different body if one thinks of it this way: what springs up from a grain of wheat is not barley, but wheat. But what makes the stalk another body from God is the way in which the decayed grain has been fortified by cultivation and enriched, so that the change is "not by abolition, but by amplification": "Cleave firmly then to the example, and keep it well in view, as a mirror of what happens to the flesh: believe that the very same *flesh* which was once sown *in death* will bear fruit in *resurrection-life*—the same in essence, only more full and perfect; not another, although reappearing in another form. For it shall receive in itself the grace and ornament which God shall please to spread over it, according to its merits."[42]

The difference is one of glory, not of substance. Tertullian amplifies his argument in a masterful way as he explains the difference between nonexistence and change:

> Now, things which are absolutely different as mutation and destruction are, will not admit mixture and confusion; in their operations, too, they differ. One destroys, the other changes. Therefore, as that which is destroyed is not changed, so that which is changed is not destroyed. To perish is altogether to cease to be what a thing once was, whereas to be changed is to exist in another condition. Now,

if a thing exists in another condition, it can still be the same thing itself; for since it does not perish, it has its existence still. A change, indeed, it has experienced, but not a destruction. A thing may undergo a complete change, and yet remain still the same thing. In like manner, a man also may be quite himself in substance even in the present life, and for all that undergo various changes—in habit, in bodily bulk, in health, in condition, in dignity, and in age—in taste, business, means, houses, laws and customs—and still lose nothing of his human nature, nor so to be made another man as to cease to be the same; indeed, I ought hardly to say another man, but another thing. This form of change even the holy Scriptures give us instances of [in the changed hand and the changed face of Moses (Exodus 4, 34), Stephen (Acts 6–7), and Jesus's Transfiguration (Matthew 17)]. So likewise changes, conversions, and reformations will necessarily take place to bring about the resurrection, but the substance *of the flesh* will still be preserved safe.[43]

As if to reinforce his perspective, Tertullian addresses the objection that if the selfsame body is raised, then will the blind, lame, and diseased be raised the same? He answers: "If we are changed for glory, how much for integrity! Any losses sustained by our bodies is an accident to them, but their entirety is their natural property. In this condition we are born." In other words, our natural condition is the life that is bestowed by God, so "to nature, not to injury, are we restored; to our state by birth, not to our condition by accident, do we rise again. *If God raises not man entire, he raises not the dead.*" This unimpaired integrity is what Tertullian takes Paul to mean when the apostle writes, "the dead shall be raised incorruptible." Tertullian then offers an analogy: If a slave is manumitted with the same flesh that had been whipped, is it right for him to undergo the same sufferings? Instead, he is honored with the white robe, a gold ring, and the name and tribe and table of his patron. "Give, then, the same prerogative to God, by virtue of such a change, of reforming our condition, not our nature, by taking away from it all sufferings, and surrounding it with safeguards of protection. Thus our flesh shall remain even after the resurrection—so far indeed susceptible of suffering, as it is the flesh, and the same flesh too; but at the same time impassable, inasmuch as it has been liberated by the Lord for the very end and purpose of being no longer capable of enduring suffering."[44]

Gregory of Nyssa would applaud Tertullian's reasoning, but he couches his argument in the context of the Orthodox tradition's emphasis on God's original design to create humans in God's image and its emphasis on the destructive nature of the passions (such as we find in Gregory's contemporary, Evagrius Ponticus). Gregory insists that the resurrection is "the reconstitution of our nature in its original form." In that form there was no age, infancy, sufferings, nor any bodily afflictions. God did not author these; these are the result of the Fall. If we travel through ice, we get chilled, through hot sun, we get burned. But if the cause is removed, the effect is gone. So it follows that our nature has to deal with passion, "but when it shall have started back to that state of passionless blessedness, it will no longer encounter the inevitable results of evil tendencies. Seeing, then, that all the infusions of the life of the brute into our nature were not in us before our humanity descended through the touch of evil into passions, most certainly, when we abandon those passions, we shall abandon all their visible results. No one, therefore, will be justified in seeking in that other life for the consequences in us of any passion."[45]

Granted, then, that though our bodies will be changed, they remain *our* bodies, a further question arises about the nature of these bodies in that these early Christian thinkers wondered what we will do with our bodies if we do not marry, engage in sexual intercourse, conceive, eat, defecate, grow, age, work, disease, and die. (These are all assumptions Gregory makes about the life after life after death.) Presumably we will have no need for teeth, heart, lungs, stomach, genitals, and feet. Gregory understands that it is logical to assume that our bodies would not include such parts if there was no need for their functions, but he also realizes that then there would not be a true resurrection of our *bodies*, so he leaves it up to "the hidden treasure-rooms of Wisdom" for the time being.[46]

Others were not as agnostic. A couple centuries before Gregory, Justin wondered whether bodies will have wombs in the case of resurrected females, and penises in the case of resurrected males. He concluded that they will, but that they did not have to function as they do now, something that is obvious in present circumstances among barren women and those who choose virginity. Contrary to Gregory's thought, food, drink, and clothing will still be necessary, as they are conditions of the flesh, but this is not so with sexual function.[47]

Tertullian strikes a similar chord. He recognizes that there will be no more use for stomachs, genitals, and limbs, but he cites voluntary eunuchs, virgins espoused to Christ, the fasts of Moses and Elijah, and sterile men and women to make the case that even though the functions and pleasures of body parts might be suspended, we might still have desires when our salvation is secure. A shipowner might repair a ship that has crashed and choose not to take it on any future voyages, but that does not mean it is useless; it still exists, so it might still have something to do, just as there will be no idleness in the presence of God. And Tertullian adds this: although our body parts will be freed from their services and no longer wanted, they must be preserved for the sake of judgment, "that everyone may receive the things done in his body." For the judgment seat of God requires that man be kept entire.[48]

Augustine might agree with Justin in one respect. Arguing that our essential nature will be preserved though defects will be removed, he concluded that females will no longer have a need for intercourse and childbirth, but the female organs will be "part of a new beauty, which will not excite the lust of the beholder . . . but will arouse the praises of God for his wisdom and compassion, in that he not only created out of nothing but freed from corruption that which he had created."[49]

Such a comment might not be Augustine's finest hour when it comes to his discussion of the removal of "defects" in the resurrected body, but he does better when he discusses with eloquence defects with regard to the martyrs. Their bodies will be whole, but they will retain the scars of their martyrdom as badges of honor.[50]

Universally,[51] Christians say that all the dead will be raised in the resurrection, but to what? On the one hand, it would be tempting to say that they are raised to divine judgment because there is a concern for divine justice and faithfulness. But there is at least one exception. Athenagoras has a somewhat strange argument that justice is not the primary reason for the resurrection. He argues that, although all who die rise again, the cause of the resurrection is not the Judgment, for not all who rise again *are* to be judged: "For if only a just judgment were the cause of the resurrection, it would of course follow that those who had done neither evil nor good—namely, very young children—would not rise again; but seeing that all are to rise again, those who have died in infancy as well as others, they too justify our conclusion that the resurrection takes place not for the sake of the judgment as the primary reason, but in consequence of the purpose of God in forming men, and the nature of the beings so formed."[52]

Athenagoras later argues that God's judgment—reward or punishment—for the way humans have lived their lives "derives its force from the end of their existence." This we expect from God's oversight for creation, "for all created things require the attention of the Creator, and each one in particular, according to its nature and the end for which it was made."[53]

Tertullian speaks more stridently of judgment, it seems. And he definitely dismisses any notion of annihilationism. At one point he asserts, "If, therefore, anyone shall violently suppose that the destruction of the soul and the flesh in hell amounts to a final annihilation of the two substances, and not to their penal treatment (as if they were to be consumed, not punished), let him recollect that the fire of hell is eternal—expressly announced as an everlasting penalty."[54]

So reward or punishment is the normal answer. But not all agree that we are raised to eternal judgment. Notably, Gregory of Nyssa argues that, based on the amount of the "ingrained wickedness of each," God will compute the duration of the cure, which cannot be achieved apart from excruciating conditions.[55] At one point, working with the analogy of the temple and its regulations in the Old Testament, Gregory refers to a time in the resurrection when

> all the further barriers by which our sin has fenced us off from the things within the veil are in the end to be taken down ... [and] all the inveterate corruption of sin has vanished from the world, then a universal feast will be kept around the Deity by those who have decorated themselves in the resurrection; and one and the same banquet will be spread for all, with no differences cutting off any rational creature from an equal participation; for those who are now excluded by reason of their sin will at last be admitted within the holiest place of God's blessing this, and will bind themselves to the horns of the Altar there, that is, to the most excellent of the transcendent powers.[56]

This all makes sense to a theologian who has insisted that God created us in the first place for incorruption, honor, power, and glory. And God's plan will not be thwarted. So when the healing process has been worked out by the fire, and sin and evil have been utterly purged, "then every one of the things which make up our conception of the good will come to take their place; incorruption, that is, and life, and order, and grace, and glory, and everything else that we conjecture is to be seen in God, and in His image, man as he was made."[57]

So whatever judgment there is must involve *both* body and soul. For instance, the way Athenagoras explains it is that humans were made body and soul, so their nature requires food and sex (to propagate the race) *and* judgment (reason) so that "food and posterity may be according to law." We are accountable for the inclinations of the body having to do with food and pleasure, but the body is not to be blamed for not being able to make distinctions, which is the function of the soul. So we are to be judged as *both* body and soul.[58] And this is to be expected because there is a chorus of voices insisting on a psychosomatic unity of the human as God has created it and as it will be resurrected.[59] As Athanagoras pointed out, if we are not raised *both* soul *and* body, we are not raised: "Man, therefore, who consists of the two parts, must continue forever. But it is impossible for him to continue unless he rise again. For if no resurrection were to take place, the nature of men as men would not continue. And if the nature of man does not continue," then all that humans are as soul and body is in vain. "But if vanity is utterly excluded from all the works of God, and from all the gifts bestowed by him, the conclusion is unavoidable, that, along with the interminable duration of the soul, there will be a perpetual continuance of the body according to its proper nature."[60]

At this point one might ask how these early Christian thinkers can affirm a *bodily* resurrection when the Apostle Paul declares in 1 Corinthians 15:50 that "flesh and blood" do not inherit eternal life. There is consensus among many of these that Paul was not speaking of bodily flesh but of the *works* of the flesh. Tertullian puts it well: "For not that is condemned in which evil is done, but only the evil which is done in it. To administer poison is a crime, but the cup in which it is given is not guilty. So the body is the vessel of the works of the flesh, whilst the soul which is within it mixes the poison of a wicked act."[61] As he says elsewhere, "Flesh and blood are excluded from the kingdom of God in respect of their sin, not of their substance."[62]

Two remaining topics deserve to be mentioned.

It has been suggested that millenarian expectations waned as the centuries retreated from the New Testament church's expressed hopes. But they were very much alive in the first two centuries of discussions about death and the resurrection. Irenaeus provides a good example as he describes the millennial kingdom—the renewed creation—in *Against Heresies*. This has nothing to do with "supercelestial matters" but with this earth and the new Jerusalem descending from above, of which the former Jerusalem is an image in which the righteous are disciplined before incorruption.[63]

In this manner, the Church inherits what was promised to Abraham—namely, the creation. The sequence and description is outlined by Irenaeus:

> [The] resurrection of the just, which takes place after the coming of Antichrist, and the destruction of all nations under his rule; in [the times of] which [resurrection] the righteous shall reign in the earth, waxing stronger by the sight of the Lord: and through Him they shall become accustomed to partake in the glory of God the Father, and shall enjoy in the kingdom intercourse and communion with the holy angels, and union with spiritual beings; and [with respect to] those whom the Lord shall find in the flesh, awaiting Him from heaven, and who have suffered tribulation, as well as escaped the hands of the Wicked one. For it is in reference to them that the prophet says: "And those that are left shall multiply upon the earth."[64]

Finally, we must mention that these same earlier theologians teach something of an interim location of those who have died and await the resurrection. Irenaeus teaches that just as Christ descended to the place of the dead before his resurrection and ascension, so his disciples will go away into the "invisible place allotted to them by God, and there remain until the resurrection." At the resurrection they will receive their bodies and come into the presence of God.[65] For Tertullian, this future resurrection is also the time of the Final Judgment; in the meantime, the flesh departs for awhile, "absorbed once more, as it were, by [mother earth's] secret embraces, ultimately to stand forth to view, like Adam when summoned to hear from his Lord and Creator the words, 'Behold, the man is become as one of us!'" only this time escaping the evil and acquiring the good.[66] Curiously, in another place Tertullian makes a distinction between the resurrection of the flesh and its *subsequent* rendering to be fit for the kingdom of God. In other words, first the flesh changes into "something else"—the incorruptible and immortal body which God gives it—and *then* it will obtain the Kingdom of God.[67]

Regarding this intermediate period, though, Bynum notes that early Christians thought of the resurrected body as the person, sleeping in the dust between death and resurrection. Only later did late antiquity Christians believe the soul continued to exist while the body was what fell and must rise again. This evolution of thought makes sense: as the expected millennial kingdom seemed further off in the distance, Christians began to realize that that body that *was* the person had to wait longer for vivification in the resurrection, encouraging the need for something to remain in the meantime—namely, that immortal component called "soul."[68]

NOTES

1. Augustine, *Concerning the City of God against the Pagans*, trans. Henry Bettenson (New York: Penguin Books, repr. 1984), 22.12.
2. Macrina's voice is actually heard in Gregory of Nyssa's treatise on the resurrection to which we will be referring. I will simply attribute what is in the treatise to Gregory, though it is assumed that Macrina is often the speaker.
3. This point is made several times in Joanne E. McWilliam Dewart, *Death and Resurrection: Message of the Fathers of the Church*, vol. 22 (Wilmington, DE: Michael Glazier, 1986).
4. Echoing Paul's argument in 1 Corinthians 15, Tertullian concludes, "If, therefore, we are to rise again after the example of Christ, who rose in the flesh, we shall certainly not rise according to that example, unless we also shall ourselves rise again in the flesh." *On the Resurrection of the Flesh*, in *The Ante-Nicene Fathers: Translations of the Writings of the Fathers Down to A.D. 325*, ed. Alexander Roberts and James Donaldson, 10 vols. (1885–1887), 48.
5. Justin, *On the Resurrection*, 9.
6. Epistle of Ignatius to the Smyrneans, 3.
7. Justin, *On the Resurrection*, 2.
8. Tertullian, *On the Resurrection of the Flesh*, 63. Typically for Irenaeus, he uses theme of recapitulation to insist that the Word took upon himself flesh of the same substance as ours in order to save *our* flesh. *Against Heresies*, 5.14.
9. Tertullian, chapter 51, in *On the Resurrection of the Flesh*, 3. Elsewhere, Tertullian says, "And so the flesh shall rise again, wholly in every man, in its own

identity, in its absolute integrity. Wherever it may be, it is in safekeeping in God's presence, through that most faithful 'Mediator between God and man (the man) Jesus Christ,' who shall reconcile both God to man and man to God; the spirit to the flesh, and the flesh to the spirit." Tertullian, *On the Resurrection of the Flesh*, 63.

10. Athenagoras, *The Resurrection of the Dead*, 3.

11. Athenagoras, *The Resurrection of the Dead*, 13.

12. Justin, *On the Resurrection*, 7–8.

13. Irenaeus, *Against Heresies*, 5.4.2. "But that He is powerful in all these respects, we ought to perceive from our origin, inasmuch as God, taking dust from the earth, formed man. And sure it is much more difficult and incredible, from non-existent bones, and nerves, and veins, and the rest of man's organization, to bring it about that all this should be, and to make man an animated and rational creature, than to reintegrate again that which had been created and then afterwards decomposed into earth, . . . having thus passed into those [elements] from which man, who had no previous existence, was formed. . . . And, therefore, since the Lord has power to infuse life into what He has fashioned, and since the flesh is capable of being quickened, what remains to prevent its participating in incorruption, which is a blissful and never-ending life granted by God?" Irenaeus, *Against Heresies*, 3.2, 3. At one point, Irenaeus appeals to the Valley of Dry Bones passage in Ezekiel 37 to make his point; see *Against Heresies*, 5.15.1. Tertullian makes nearly the same argument as Irenaeus: "For if God produced all things whatever out of nothing, He will be able to draw forth from nothing even the flesh which had fallen into nothing. . . . And surely He is most competent to re-create who created, inasmuch as it is a far greater work to have produced than to have reproduced, to have imparted a beginning, than to have maintained a continuance. On this principle, you may quite sure that the restoration of the flesh is easier than its first formation." Tertullian, *On the Resurrection of the Flesh*, 11.

14. Augustine, *City of God*, 22.20.

15. For example, see 1 Clement 24–26; Justin, *On the Resurrection*, 5; Tatian, *To the Greeks*, 6; Athenagoras, *The Resurrection of the Dead*, 16; Tertullian, *On the Resurrection of the Flesh*, 12–13. As do others, Tertullian (in chapter 58) also reminds us of biblical examples that inspire us, including Jonah, Enoch, Elijah, and the three Hebrews in the fire. Theophilus includes many

of the examples we have mentioned and even a seed that a bird swallows and leaves through defecation so that a tree grows up. See Theophilus to Autolycus, 13.

16. For example, see Irenaeus, *Against Heresies*, 5.7.2; Tertullian, *Against Marcion*, 5.10; Origen, *De Principiis*, 2.10.3; Athenagoras, *The Resurrection of the Dead*, 16; Gregory of Nyssa, *On the Soul and the Resurrection*, 446, 466–68. While she recognizes that the seed is the oldest and continuously present Christian metaphor for the resurrection of the body, Bynum insists that "the seed metaphor is not the major image in patristic and medieval discussions of eschatology." See Caroline Walker Bynum, *The Resurrection of the Body in Western Christianity, 200–1336* (New York: Columbia University Press, 1995), 3, 6, 13.

17. For this and what follows, see Gregory of Nyssa, *On the Soul and the Resurrection*, 466–68.

18. Athenagoras, *The Resurrection of the Dead*, 12, 16.

19. Gregory of Nyssa argues against those who teach reincarnation or transmigration of souls, such as the Pythagoreans, later Platonists, Origen, or the *Phaedo* teach.

20. Bynum, *Resurrection*, 11; also 112–13.

21. Bynum, *Resurrection*, 24–25.

22. Citing the three resurrections Jesus performed (Mark 5:22; Luke 7:12; and John 9:30), Irenaeus makes this point in *Against Heresies*, 5.13.1; Athenagoras is just as insistent; see *The Resurrection of the Dead*, 25.

23. Gregory of Nyssa, *On the Soul and the Resurrection*, 463.

24. Gregory of Nyssa, *On the Soul and the Resurrection*, 463.

25. Gregory of Nyssa, *On the Soul and the Resurrection*, 448.

26. Gregory of Nyssa, *On the Soul and the Resurrection*, 454–59. In these pages he also argues against what is essentially Gnosticism, chiding those who practice it by suggesting that "evil controls the creation of all beings," especially in the Spring when "the large majority of the brute creation copulate," so that souls have bodies into which to drop; then, if humans refuse to have intercourse, the souls end up being vagabonds, wandering around "houseless." He thinks that soul and body come into being and grow simultaneously, though he refuses to speculate how the soul comes into being; and he believes there is a plentitude of humans that will be reached at some point.

27. The above is taken from Gregory of Nyssa, *On the Making of Man*, 27.2–5 and *On the Soul and the Resurrection*, 445–46. In the latter (on page 446), Gregory uses a common analogy from broken vessels and the potter: "the individual is as such a vessel; he has been moulded out of the universal matter, owing to the concourse of his atoms; and he exhibits in a form peculiarly his own a marked distinction from his kind; and when that form has gone to pieces the soul that has been mistress of this particular vessel will have an exact knowledge of it, derived even from its fragments; nor will she leave this property, either, in the common blending with all the other fragments, or if it be plunged into the still formless part of the matter from which the atoms have come; she always remembers her own as it was when compact in bodily form, and after dissolution she never makes any mistake about it, led by marks still clinging to the remains."

28. Augustine, *Faith, Hope and Charity*, 23.88.

29. See Augustine, *City of God*, 22.14, 20.

30. Augustine, *City of God*, 22.19; *Faith, Hope and Charity*, 23.89. Augustine was not the first nor the only one to use this analogy. It was used much earlier, for example, by Justin, who found confirmation even among Platonists, Stoics, and Epicureans that just as an artificer can remake something of clay or wax or mosaic tiles collected from the very same composition as before, "shall not God be able to collect again the decomposed members of the flesh, and make the same body as was formerly produced by Him?" Justin, *On the Resurrection*, 6.

31. Augustine, *Faith, Hope and Charity*, 23.85.

32. Augustine, *Faith, Hope and Charity*, 23.87. Justin bases his claim that resurrected bodies will not have the defects that they have had in this life by referencing Jesus's miracles: "For if on earth He healed the sicknesses of the flesh, and made the body whole, much more will He do this in the resurrection, so that the flesh shall rise perfect and entire" Justin, *On the Resurrection*, 4.

33. Augustine, *City of God*, 22.14.

34. Augustine, *Faith, Hope and Charity*, 23.90; *City of God*, 22.19.

35. Augustine, *Faith, Hope and Charity*, 23.92.

36. Augustine, *City of God*, 22.19.

37. Augustine, *City of God*, 22.15–16.

38. Augustine, *Faith, Hope and Charity*, 23.92.

39. Athenagoras, *The Resurrection of the Dead*, 7.

40. Athenagoras, *The Resurrection of the Dead*, 8. Tertullian argues, "But the beasts and the fishes are mentioned in relation to the restoration of flesh and blood, in order the more emphatically to express the resurrection of such bodies as have even been devoured, when redress is said to be demanded of their very devourers." Tertullian, *On the Resurrection of the Flesh*, 32. And on this same subject matter, Augustine states: "And this man's flesh, which starvation had stripped from him, will be restored to him by the one who can bring back even what has been exhaled into the air. Indeed even if that flesh had completely disappeared, and none of its material had remained in any cranny of the natural world, the Almighty would reproduce it from what source he chose." Augustine, *City of God*, 22.20.

41. Bynum deals with this issue quite a bit in her book *The Resurrection of the Body in Western Christianity*.

42. Tertullian, *On the Resurrection of the Flesh*, 52.

43. Tertullian, *On the Resurrection of the Flesh*, 56. Gregory makes a similar argument: "You will behold this bodily envelopment, which is now dissolved in death, woven again out of the same atoms, not indeed into this organization with its gross and heavy texture, but with its threads worked up into something more subtle and ethereal, so that you will not only have near you that which you love, but it will be restored to you with a brighter and more entrancing beauty." Gregory of Nyssa, *On the Soul and the Resurrection*, 453.

44. Tertullian, *On the Resurrection of the Flesh*, 57.

45. Gregory of Nyssa, *On the Soul and the Resurrection*, 464.

46. Gregory of Nyssa, *On the Soul and the Resurrection*, 464.

47. Justin, *On the Resurrection*.

48. Tertullian, *On the Resurrection of the Flesh*, 60–61.

49. Augustine, *City of God*, 22.17.

50. Augustine, *City of God*, 22.19. See Irenaeus's comments on the resurrection of those who have been slain because of their love of God in *Against Heresies*, 5.32.1. Gregory of Nyssa's treatise *On the Soul and the Resurrection* is written presumably on the occasion of Basil's death and his and Macrina's grief. Interestingly, Bynum remarks that the early third-century AD understanding of the body seems to owe much to the context of persecution; see *On the Soul and the Resurrection*, 58.

51. For example, see Augustine, *Faith, Hope and Charity*, 23.84.
52. Athenagoras, *The Resurrection of the Dead*, 14.
53. Athenagoras, *The Resurrection of the Dead*, 18.
54. Tertullian, *On the Resurrection of the Flesh*, 35.
55. Gregory of Nyssa, *On the Soul and the Resurrection*, 465.
56. Gregory of Nyssa, *On the Soul and the Resurrection*, 461.
57. Gregory of Nyssa, *On the Soul and the Resurrection*, 468. Origen expressed the view that, while the "fire" may not be temporary, it can't destroy the resurrected body: "even the body which rises again of those who are to be destined to everlasting fire or to severe punishments, is by the very change of the resurrection so incorruptible, that it cannot be corrupted and dissolved even by severe punishments." Origen, *De Principiis*, 2.10.3.
58. Athenagoras, *The Resurrection of the Dead*, 18. See also Tertullian, *On the Resurrection of the Flesh*, 7, 14–16, 18, 34, 40, and 45, where he argues for traducianism.
59. Tertullian expresses this psychosomatic unity beautifully when he writes: "Both natures has He [Christ] already united in his own self; He has fitted them together as bride and bridegroom in the reciprocal bond of wedded life. Now, if any should insist on making the soul the bride, then the flesh will follow the soul as her dowry. The soul shall never be an outcast, to be had home by the bridegroom bare and naked. She has her dower, her outfit, her fortune in the flesh, which shall accompany her with the love and fidelity of a foster-sister. But suppose the flesh to be the bride, then in Christ Jesus she has in the contract of His blood received His Spirit as her spouse. . . . Why, then, soul, should you envy the flesh? There is none, after the Lord, whom you should love so dearly; no more like a brother to you, which is even born along with yourself and God. You ought rather to have been by your prayers obtaining resurrection for her: her sins, whatever they were, were owing to you." *On the Resurrection of the Flesh*, 63.
60. Athenagoras, *The Resurrection of the Dead*, 15. See also Justin, *On the Resurrection*, 8; Irenaeus, *Against Heresies*, 5.6.1 (the "commingling and union" of flesh, soul, and spirit all constitute the "perfect man"); Gregory of Nyssa, *On the Soul and the Resurrection*, 445.
61. Tertullian, *Against Marcion*, 5.10. See a similar interpretation in Irenaeus, *Against Heresies*, 5.9.1–4, and in Augustine, *Faith, Hope and Charity*, 23.91.
62. Tertullian, *On the Resurrection of the Flesh*, 46.

63. Irenaeus, *Against Heresies*, 5.36.1–2. Also see 5.26–35. Compare 1 Clement 23–24.

64. Irenaeus, *Against Heresies*, 5.35.1.

65. Irenaeus, *Against Heresies*, 5.31.2.

66. Tertullian, *On the Resurrection of the Flesh*, 63; see also 22–25.

67. Tertullian, *Against Marcion*, 5.10.

68. Bynum, *Resurrection*, 13–14.

Chapter 4

HEAVEN OPENED IN THE SOUL
THE RELIGIOUS IMAGINATION OF METHODISTS

David McAllister-Wilson

David McAllister-Wilson is president of Wesley Theological Seminary in Washington, DC.

What do Methodists think about what lies beyond the grave? What do we believe about the afterlife? I don't speak for the forty-eight million who call themselves "Methodist," much less the roughly five hundred million more "Wesleyan," "Nazarene," "Holiness," and "Pentecostal" peoples who descend from the Wesleyan/Methodist movement. Moreover, I am only an amateur scholar, a reader of Wesleyan theology, a preacher, an employer of theologians, and an ordained minister deeply immersed in the United Methodist branch of the tradition. Therefore, my contribution will be more journalistic and conversational than academic. From this vantage point, I want to share four insights.

The most important thing to confess is that in my community of United Methodists we do not talk about the afterlife very much. Indeed, in all my travels, the countless sermons and lectures I have heard, and all the late-night discussions I have been a part of, I recall very few in-depth or detailed speculation about life after this one—no speculation about streets paved with gold or fiery pits. So say most Methodist clergy I have queried since receiving this assignment.

Yet the very night I write these words, this entry appears on the Facebook page of a prominent clergywoman friend: "My dad died last night. Growing up between two brothers, I've spent my whole life basking in the light that is born of being a daughter. An only daughter of an amazing Dad. I think it was the love of my parents that made it so easy for me to believe in the love of our God. He often said I went into ministry to get him into heaven. And today in the absence of his voice I am praying that everything I believe about heaven is true."

Her post is an example of the common contemporary Methodist assumption about the afterlife. In my experience, Methodists seem to believe in the afterlife in the way we believe there will be life found elsewhere in the universe some day and a cure for cancer will be found: we expect so; we hope so. And our hopes are loosely derived from our belief in a wondrous creation and a loving God.

And that leads me to the second insight. Many Methodist doctrinal positions are exercises in what John Wesley called "practical divinity."[1] They are tethered to a classical Protestant theological superstructure, but the tether is long and flexible. This is due both to the synthetic and experimental nature of John Wesley as a theologian and our belief in the pervasive (we call it prevenient) work of the Holy Spirit. We are more inductive than deductive in our theological reasoning. This isn't to say that we lack doctrinal norms. Rather, we think the proof is in the eating of the pudding, and we "test the spirits" to see if they are of God for our time and circumstance. Perhaps this is why, although every seminarian studies formal soteriology and eschatology as topics in a course in systematic theology, the specific details of the ultimate consequences of sin and death or of the eternal life in Christ are more likely to be discussed in pastoral care or liturgy courses. And so our professional beliefs on the subject are ad hoc, shaped by the need to console the dying and their loved ones.

And this leads me to the third insight. When it comes to the afterlife, much is left to individual contemplation. And today, heaven (or hell, for that matter) exists in the peripheral vision of Methodist religious imagination. It has not always been so. This can be seen by the only entry requirement for the movement set forth by the founder, John Wesley, in the "General Rules of the United Societies." One needed *only* a "desire to flee from the wrath to come, to be saved from their sins."[2] This reads like a doctrinal litmus test. But it is more instructive to observe it presupposes a shared religious sensibility, a deeply embedded supposition about the "undiscovered country from whose bourn no traveler returns."[3] It was assumed everyone had this desire. They could just as well have said, "Everyone is welcome."

The fourth insight is that in practice, Methodists appear to have what is sometimes called a "realized eschatology." The term itself arises early in the twentieth-century theological lexicon, but the distinction is much older and concerns the meaning of Jesus's teaching regarding the kingdom of God. Was he—is he—speaking of something to come at the end of time or something already here, as in "The kingdom of God is at hand" (Mark 1:15 Revised Standard Version)? I will discuss some of the complications of this question later, but at this point it is important to say, for Wesley, salvation is not just a onetime transaction in the present for that time in the future when we enter the kingdom. In his sermon "The Scripture Way of Salvation,"[4] he says, "It is not something at a distance; it is a present thing; a blessing which, through the free mercy of God, ye are now in possession of." And in "The Way to the Kingdom," he uses the wonderfully evocative phrase "Heaven opened in the soul:"

> This holiness and happiness, joined in one, are sometimes styled, in the inspired writings, "the kingdom of God," (as by our Lord in the text,) and sometimes, "the kingdom of heaven." It is termed "the kingdom of God," because it is the immediate fruit of God's reigning in the soul. So soon as ever he takes unto himself his mighty power, and sets up his throne in our hearts, they are instantly filled with this "righteousness, and peace, and joy in the Holy Ghost." It

is called "the kingdom of heaven" because it is (in a degree) heaven opened in the soul. For whosoever they are that experience this, they can aver before angels and men.[5]

"Heaven opened in the soul." The immanence of God through the sanctifying work of the Holy Spirit, the in-breaking of the kingdom of God, looms large in the Methodist religious imagination. Surely, it accounts for our founding of organizations like the Salvation Army and Goodwill Industries, and for the fact that we have established so many colleges and hospitals and other institutions for human flourishing. We join in the widely used Memorial Acclamation in the Eucharistic rite: "Christ has died, Christ is risen, Christ will come again." But "Christ is risen" seems to be our field of focus, which has the effect of moving the afterlife into the background.

However, if we leave it there, we sell our tradition short and impoverish our religious vision, leaving us unprepared to face the existential questions of life and death with anything more than ungrounded platitudes. I will attempt to describe the theology that funded the Methodist understanding of the last things in John Wesley's time and later in nineteenth-century America. I will conclude by offering a proposition for how we can recover the essence of our tradition in a way that addresses what I believe is the modern version of the "fear of the wrath to come" that underlies our current unarticulated understanding of what lies beyond the grave.

What do Methodists believe, and how do we come to believe it? The precursor for Methodism is, in many respects, Jacobus Arminius (1560–1609), and his name lived on in Methodism for generations as a way to establish a contrast with the descendants of Calvinism. (By the way, many have suggested that Latter-day Saint theology is in this same "Arminian" family). But certainly, the formative period for Methodist theology is the life and work of John Wesley (1703–91) and Charles Wesley (1707–88). What they together developed is less a set of doctrines than a field guide for a movement in the form of sermons, hymns, and rules. Ryan Danker, assistant professor of history of Christianity and Methodist studies at Wesley Seminary, argues the Wesleys didn't present a full theological system for two reasons: "(1) they were Anglicans and so they did theology (or rather divinity) as Anglicans always did; through prayers, ritual, homilies, and treatises very similar to the way the early church did theology (as opposed to the scholastics and continental systematicians), and (2) because they assumed that Methodism would be built upon the larger catholic structure provided by English Christianity."[6]

Methodism is often referred to as a "religion of the heart," situated in the Pietist stream of Protestantism. However, it is not a "heart" religion at the expense of the "head." The Wesleys did not reject logical reasoning, nor were they impulsive or antinomian. Wesleyanism is an "experiential" faith but in the eighteenth-century sense of that word. It is experimental and empirical. The Wesleys were very much educated men of their time that were fascinated by the early stages of scientific exploration. John's journals indicate that he kept up with discoveries in medicine, chemistry, astronomy, and electricity. In that spirit of curiosity, John Wesley's theology was practical (it had to actually work), and it was speculative—not speculative in the sense of being imaginative but in the sense of building on previous work, examining the evidence, and putting forth hypotheses to advance scientific understanding.

Allow me this analogy. Just as his contemporary Benjamin Franklin made the connection between the power of lightning from the heavens and electrical activity on earth, John was conducting experiments on the power emanating from heaven—the grace of God—and how that power can be experienced. No doubt, had he known of the pervasiveness of electricity, even to the cellular and atomic level, he would have found even more confirmation of his hypothesis that grace is infused in all creation. To use the language of Wesley's Anglican theology, it is "prevenient." He was seeking the experience of grace made known by the love of God in the lives of the people in the movement. This is the way to understand how Wesleyanism is "experiential" and a "heart religion."

The salient feature of the Wesleys' understanding of what lies beyond the grave is their discovery that God's love is readily available, that it has the power to transform, and that the growth and sharing of this love is the essence of a sanctified life. And by logical extension, they believed this boundless and expanding love will triumph at the end of life and the end of time.

What becomes more difficult and rather esoteric to our contemporary ears is John Wesley's understanding of the timeline of the afterlife. The questions follow: When will Christ return and where does that event fit relative to his thousand-year (millennial) reign spoken of in Revelation 20:1–6? And what is the experience of the soul during this time? Randy Maddox concludes Wesley began "amillennialist," flirted with premillennialism, and ended up postmilliennialist because it fit well with his "progressive eschatology."[7] Underlying everything else to say about a Methodist understanding of what lies beyond the grave is while in practice we often appear to have a "realized eschatology," our tradition is a "progressive eschatology" because Wesley believed we are living in a dispensation of time when grace is a particularly active and growing presence.

There was nothing inherently new in this concept. Rather, Wesley's contribution is the way he puts classic doctrine together. There are five elements from the received tradition in Wesley's progressive vision of the procession of God's redeeming love. One is a perfunctory acceptance of the ancient cosmology of "three heavens," with the lower two referring to earth and sky and the uppermost being the "immediate residence" of God on a throne accompanied by winged angels and archangels.[8] A second is the immortality of the soul despite its fall in sin.[9] A third is an understanding of an intermediate state prior to the general resurrection and final judgment at the end of the story of the old creation that entails a bodily resurrection. What is distinctive is how he winds his way around these concepts like pylons on an obstacle course—focusing on the way God's grace works, practically, in the lives of men and women—and explicating an existing doctrine of the threefold sequence of the work of grace: prevenience, justifying, and sanctifying.

What course does he follow? Let's begin with the end in mind. The New Creation, as described in a John Wesley sermon by that name, is an ecstatic vision of the general resurrection involving perfected forms of the current created order: no comets, only perfect stars; no thorns or thistles; no storms in land or water; and no danger of harm from animals—to cite only a few examples of perfected creation. As for the experience of the immortal soul, it is a deeply comforting vision of communion with the triune God:

> Hence will arise an unmixed state of holiness and happiness far superior to that which Adam enjoyed in Paradise. In how beautiful a manner is this described by the Apostle: "God shall wipe away all tears from their eyes; and there shall be no more death, neither sorrow, nor crying, neither shall there be any more pain: For the former things are done away!" As there will be no more death, and no more pain or sickness preparatory thereto; as there will be no more grieving for, or parting with, friends; so there will be no more sorrow or crying. Nay, but there will be a greater deliverance than all this; for there will be no more sin. And, to crown all, there will be a deep, an intimate, an uninterrupted union with God; a constant communion with the Father and his Son Jesus Christ, through the Spirit; a continual enjoyment of the Three-One God, and of all the creatures in him![10]

In truth, while the details of the vision have scriptural moorings, they are not being proffered as doctrine. They are best understood as useful to the religious imagination, much as C. S. Lewis would later do in the Chronicles of Narnia. And as with Lewis, John's vision supports the doctrinal point that a wonderful consummation lies at the end of a progressive eschatology with the love of God as its constant motive. Consider how his brother Charles used the phrase "new creation" in one of his most popular hymns, "Love Divine, All Loves Excelling":

Finish, then, thy new creation; pure and spotless let us be.
Let us see Thy great salvation perfectly restored in Thee;
Changed from glory into glory, till in heaven we take our place,
Till we cast our crowns before Thee, Lost in wonder, love, and
praise.[11]

Granted, this hymn is about the transformation of individuals as "new creations" in life, but it captures the eschatological vision of the experience, to be "lost in wonder, love, and praise." The Wesleys saw the salvation story of scripture being experienced in the movement as evidence of the love of God. Indeed, they saw the movement of the Holy Spirit among a group of people "desiring to flee the wrath to come," who experienced this love as an assurance of salvation, which grew into love of God and neighbor. And they understood this movement to be unfolding in history, thus, *progressive* eschatology. They saw Christ working through his Church to recover the lost and foster their growth in grace as a step in the reclamation of the whole of the fallen creation. As such, it had immediate consequences—fruits—in the way this love was expressed in acts of mercy and justice. Later, this important element of their work tends to stand alone as a *realized* eschatology, removed from its place in a comprehensive plan of salvation, but the Wesleys would have rejected this as both unscriptural and impotent.

The driving force of this progressive reclamation project is the Methodist doctrine of "perfection." At the early Methodist conferences, all the clergy were asked an important question each year: "Do you believe you can attain perfection in love in this life; are you earnestly striving for it?"[12] We are still asked that by the bishop in the service of ordination. To seek "perfection in love" implies a constant striving toward an ideal state. Hear this urging John Wesley provides in his sermon "On Faith," and notice also the dynamic imperative:

Go on to perfection. Yea, and when ye have attained a measure of perfect love, when God has circumcised your hearts, and enabled you to love him with all your heart and with all your soul, think not of resting there. That is impossible. You cannot stand still;

you must either rise or fall; rise higher or fail lower. Therefore the voice of God to the children of Israel, to the children of God, is, "Go forward!" Forgetting the things that are behind, and reaching forward unto those that are before, press on to the mark, for the prize of your high calling of God in Christ Jesus![13]

"You must either rise or fall." It sounds like the second week of a gym membership. Indeed, in contrast to the Calvinists, to some degree, Wesley believed we "work out our own salvation," described in a sermon by that name.[14] The work of sanctifying grace is interactive, cooperant, and "responsible," to use Maddox's term. And so, in addition to those who resist the work of God's justifying grace, it is possible to fall from grace and join those who suffer the final judgment. But as this passage indicates, even though you may at a moment in your life be justified, the work of grace is not finished, and, to some degree, it is on you—"you must either rise or fall." This entails even the possibility of losing salvation. He lays this case out in "Predestination Calmly Considered."[15]

In his sermon "Of Hell," John Wesley describes the awful consequences, the Final Judgment on those who fall from grace or refuse to accept it. Similar to his description of the New Creation, he describes the torment in exquisite detail. Speculative scientist as he is, he even suggests from the example of woven asbestos (which, he says, can be found in the British Museum) how it is the fires of hell can burn and not consume.[16]

In this sermon, and elsewhere, Wesley describes the most interesting and illuminating aspect of his understanding of what happens to all souls—saved and damned—beyond the grave. We return to the problem of timing and sequence, and the critical question is about the period in time as we experience it between the death of the individual body and the general resurrection and establishment of the new creation—the "new heaven and new earth" of the book of Revelation. I wonder how the scientist in Wesley would have appropriated new understandings of the relationship between space and time and Heisenberg's uncertainty principle, but what Wesley had to choose from were varying theological cosmologies in the received tradition.

The first thing to say is that Wesley had a full-throated defense of the bodily resurrection. As he says in his sermon "On the Resurrection of the Dead," "The plain notion of a resurrection requires, that the self-same body that died should rise again. Nothing can be said to be raised again, but that very body that died. If God give to our souls at the last day a new body, this cannot be called the resurrection of our body; because that word plainly implies the fresh production of what was before."[17] And he speculates on the same "practical" questions those before and after have raised about this doctrine:

> God can distinguish and keep unmixed from all other bodies the particular dust into which our several bodies are dissolved, and can gather it together and join it again, how far soever dispersed asunder. God is infinite both in knowledge and power. He knoweth the number of the stars, and calleth them all by their names; he can tell the number of the sands on the sea-shore: And is it at all incredible, that He should distinctly know the several particles of dust into which the bodies of men are mouldered, and plainly discern to whom they belong, and the various changes they have undergone? Why should it be thought strange, that He, who at the first formed us, whose eyes saw our substance yet being imperfect, from whom we were not hid when we were made in secret, and curiously wrought in the lowest parts of the earth, should know every part of our bodies, and every particle of dust whereof we were composed?[18]

However, Wesley did not believe that these souls simply "sleep" awaiting the new creation. And he did not believe in the Roman Catholic doctrine of purgatory because he could not find scriptural warrant for this notion, and frankly it conflicted with his theological project. In his scheme, it was essential that the final judgment as to the disposition of the soul occurred at the death of the physical body—no remediation in purgatory. However, he did still have to consider the problem of this

intermediate period before the new creation. His solution is to appropriate the tradition of "paradise" or "Hades" as the antechamber of heaven,
or precisely, two regions—paradise as the antechamber of heaven; Hades
as the antechamber of hell.

In "On Hell,"[19] he describes the experience of the damned. They are
aware of what they have lost in the sense of the earthly sensations and
joys and what they have lost going forward—the possibility of joining
with God in heaven. On the other hand, in the other room, Wesley's
description of paradise is characteristic of his entire theological vision.
Here, on the "porch of heaven . . . the spirits of just men are made perfect.
It is in heaven only that there is the fullness of joy; the pleasures that
are at God's right hand for evermore."[20] As Ken Collins describes it,
"Wesley imagines an idyllic picture where all the saints will be 'convers-
ing with all the wise and holy souls that have lived in all ages and nations
. . .' With this increase in knowledge will also come an advance in happiness and holiness, whereby the saints will be 'continually ripened for
heaven.'"[21] Here is the penultimate moment in his progressive eschatology. Wesleyan emphasis on sanctification and Christian perfection
extended beyond the grave, but now, in the antechamber of paradise, it
is occurring without the fear of falling back into sin, a continuation of
growth toward perfection in love.

What is most beguiling about this vision is the communal experience. Frank Baker, in his examination of Charles Wesley's hymns, says
that "heaven for Charles Wesley was not simply a place of rest—or even
of joy—after death. Heaven was a relationship between God and man, a
relationship summed up in the word 'love.'"[22] It is not always clear with
Charles (or John, for that matter) when they are talking about "heaven"
or "paradise." But if he accepts John's timeline, the closing words of his
hymn "One Church, Above, Beneath" is singing about paradise and the
ancient doctrine of communion of the Saints, those in heaven and on
earth:

> Come let us join our Friends above
> That have obtain'd the prize,

And on the eagle-wings of love
To joy celestial rise;
Let all the Saints terrestrial sing
With those to glory gone,
For all the servants of our King
In earth and Heaven are one.[23]

It must be said that Charles through his sermons had a longer impact on the religious imagination of the Methodists than did John through his sermons, letters, rules and other writings. Certainly that is because music and singing penetrates the soul and gives us a sense that we are joining a heavenly choir. But also Charles wrote from a richer life experience. Many have observed that, while John had a failed marriage and no children and was probably not much fun to be around, Charles had the experience of a loving family life, which also entailed great personal grief. The death of his son, for example, produces poetry of great anguish. For generations, parents have sung his hymns with tears in their eyes.

In his more than six thousand hymn texts, many deal with death and the afterlife. And, while to modern ears, they sometimes sound like whistling past the graveyard, in fact, they give voice to the vibrant vision of paradise and the new creation. The text, "On the Corpse of a Believer," for instance: "Ah! Lovely Appearance of Death! No Sight upon Earth is so fair: Not all the gay Pageants that breathe can with a dead Body compare."[24]

David Hempton observes that much can be learned about foundational Methodist spirituality from their attitude about death. He points out the "Methodist *Arminian Magazine* carried far more accounts of deathbed scenes than its Calvinist rival, The Gospel Magazine." As proclamation, prescription and persuasion, Hempton says, "There was no more appropriate place to preach the Methodist message of fleeing from the wrath to come than the attended deathbed."[25]

As vivid and interesting as the foregoing may be, it must be acknowledged that, over time, much of the details of what John and Charles Wesley taught about the afterlife did not become normative for later

Methodists. What quickly broke down is the map of the territory beyond the grave. It is as if the carefully separated differentiation between paradise and the new creation, heaven and its antechamber, became one piece in the religious imagination of the nineteenth century and became like the clouds in the romantic landscape paintings of John Constable barely a generation later. Wesley Professor of Systematic Theology Kendall Soulen offers one explanation: "Methodists never have had an interest in teaching anything distinctive on this point—he would have hoped he taught in concert with the New Testament and the consensus of patristic thought, and he probably did."[26] Two well-known pieces of John's biography summarize the essence of his understanding. Often he described himself as "a brand, plucked from the fire," which has a double meaning referring to his being saved as a child from a burning building and his experience of salvation. And then on his deathbed he said on two occasions, "The best of all is, God is with us."[27]

However, the absence of formal explicit teaching did not mean the Methodists stopped imagining the experience beyond the grave—far from it. Before evaluating the contemporary scene, it is important to briefly consider the Methodist religious imagination concerning the afterlife during that momentous period after the death of the Wesleys in America during the first half of the nineteenth century. Methodist preachers were prepared by their polity, their theology, and their spiritual sensibilities to be, along with the Baptists, the primary leaders in the revival, known as the Second Great Awakening. To a significant degree, this was the second wave of Methodism, and it was very much animated by an eschatological religious imagination.

Many have grouped and labeled this profound religious movement along with trends in art and literature such as Romanticism. Today, that word has some disparaging overtones, as though it is only an irrational and sentimental movement. If one does not believe in the active work of the Holy Spirit and a vision about the meaning and future of creation, it was perhaps only "emotional." But we look on the historical record with the eyes of faith and see another force at work, a spiritual experience, which includes the emotions.

What looms largest in this formative period of Methodism is the Second Great Awakening, preeminently led by and through women. While this may appear to play to a stereotype, the more logical explanation is, in the words of Isaiah 53:3, women led lives of constant sorrow and were "acquainted with grief." As many as a third of women in the period died in childbirth, and many mothers regularly cared for their dying children. One thinks of the words of Jesus on the cross to his mother, Mary, "Woman, here is your son" (John 19:26 RSV). And, as women were there when he was crucified, they were also at the tomb as the first evangelists and the primary theologians for the Awakening.

Women were the best and most numerous primary sources for understanding the religious imagination about what could transcend death.[28] What was being searched for and found was an inner experience of assurance, the individual awareness that he or she has been saved. Central to that experience is what John Wesley described as "heaven opened in the soul," and these vivid and ecstatic visions included a strong sense of the communion of the Saints. These were often given voice in Methodist love feasts and class meetings and captured in journals and poems and hymns.[29]

From these kinds of sources, there are to be found common themes about what heaven is like. There were angels bright and saints in white. And the most important feature is that heaven is engaged in endless worship and the singing of praises. Loved ones are there and also others who have fought the battle and won. "Zion" is used to describe both the church in worship and a foretaste of the final reunion in the heavenly city. There are also vivid pictures of hell to be found, but heaven was foremost in their sight. One interesting example is this verse from Sara Jones, a Methodist from Virginia. Here, she illustrates an interesting feature in many visions of the afterlife. The figure she encounters—though certainly and logically the risen Christ—she refers to as "Jesus."

> Then on wings of angels my Jesus I'll meet
> And gaze on my treasure and fall at his feet.

With raptures of joy in glory I'll tell
That Jesus' image my spirit doth fill.[30]

Those who were even more profoundly acquainted with death and forced to contemplate eternity were African Americans. Eileen Guenther, in her book looking at the spirituals in slave life, says, "Death was always seen as a relief from the degradation and pain of slavery, a viable alternative to freedom. In that sense, death was more desired than feared."[31] Richard Allen, who later founded the African Methodist Episcopal Church described the company to be found in heaven: "When, therefore, we shall leave this impertinent and unsociable world, and all our good old friends that are gone to Heaven before us shall meet us as soon as we are landed upon the shore of eternity, and with infinite congratulations for our safe arrival, shall conduct us into the company of patriarchs, prophets, apostles and martyrs."[32]

The Awakening crossed denominational lines and ultimately created new denominations. Can we identify specifically Methodist understandings of the afterlife in this period? Among other elements, it is clear that they were still practicing a full progressive eschatology. Salvation began with the solitary anxiety of the mourner's bench, and then came the experience of assurance—the in-breaking of the kingdom in the heart—followed by a sanctified life of holiness, and going on to perfection as a foretaste of the eventual reward.

Gradually, the Second Great Awakening waned. The main body of Methodism continued to grow, even as it spawned other new movements. But this second movement of Methodism became institutionalized. And as that happened, references to the afterlife began to recede. Baker describes the process by which Charles's ecstatic vision was toned down. "The subsequent lowering of the spiritual temperature, even within Methodism, made it somewhat difficult after a few generations to sing many of Charles Wesley's greatest hymns without either hypocrisy or at least a faintly uneasy self-consciousness. . . . One example of this debasing of Wesley's spiritual currency is to be seen in his preoccupation with Heaven."[33] Baker points out in later use of his hymns, the final verse dealing with heaven is left out.

A hundred years later, what is the current state of final affairs in Methodism? As I indicated at the beginning, heaven and hell are rarely discussed. The fundamental guide for my denomination, The United Methodist Church, is the Book of Discipline, in which very little can be found on the subject of life beyond the grave. Near the beginning, as a kind of preamble, is the section entitled "Basic Christian Affirmations," which instructs, "We pray and work for the coming of God's realm and reign to the world and rejoice in the promise of everlasting life that overcomes death and the forces of evil." Also, the Articles of Religion, as adopted by the Conference of 1808, are enshrined in the Discipline. There, Article 14 rejects the "Romish doctrine" of purgatory.[34] The historic creeds are affirmed, particularly the Apostles' Creed, which affirms, "I believe in the Holy Spirit, the holy catholic and apostolic Church, the communion of saints, the forgiveness of sins, the resurrection of the body, and the life everlasting." There are several other instances of classic statements of doctrine, but no descriptions of the afterlife, nothing of the experiential religion of early centuries.

Instead, the Book of Discipline is primarily articles of incorporation and bylaws governing the earthly work of the church. And, another normative work for us is *The United Methodist Social Principles*,[35] a list of statements adopted by General Conferences. The primacy of this document underscores an earlier point that in practice we have a "realized eschatology," concerned about how the kingdom of God is being revealed in this life.

In *The United Methodist Book of Worship*, which is recommended for use by clergy as a guide in the conduct of worship and other services, it is instructive that the funeral service is entitled "A Service of Death and Resurrection." In that liturgy, our hope is directed to the general resurrection, and there are only very faint echoes of the old visions of the communion of Saints and the comforts of being with God, with none of the vivid details.[36] The specific understanding of Paradise, which was so illustrative of the earlier religious imagination, is completely lost today. To be fair, descriptions of the afterlife never had the status of doctrine in eighteenth and nineteenth centuries either. Ted A. Campbell indicates in *Methodist Doctrine: The Essentials* that we "reject the idea of purgatory but beyond that maintain silence on what lies between death and the last judgment."[37] But there is almost nothing left of any quasi-doctrinal superstructure for a coherent progressive eschatology.

On the other hand, in the absence of formal teaching, there is a "folk theology," informed more by other cultural sources as people fill in the blanks. I recently emailed a lifelong Methodist and asked what her thinking was about life after death. Almost immediately she replied with a very intimate account, which, she said, she has never told anyone in over eighty years, including the ten to fifteen pastors who have known her. My wife, Drema, who specializes in end-of-life care, reports that these privately nurtured hopes are common.

What happened? Did death drift to the periphery of religious imagination because modern medicine extended life and cut rates of the death of mother and child? That's a common explanation. Others suggest modernity and scientific rationalism have pushed these considerations underground. But it is probably more complicated. My Methodist clergy colleagues in West Africa report that mention of the afterlife is rare there as well despite their experience with war and disease. They explain that African spirituality has its own religious imagination about the temporal presence of the ancestors and the immanence of the spirit world. So, the "afterlife," isn't "after," it is present among us. Indeed, hours before I write this sentence, I sat in a formal, high church memorial service in Boston, and two of the eulogists spoke of the deceased as if he were in the room listening.

Does it matter that Methodists have lost a common, explicit, and theologically grounded religious imagination regarding the afterlife? At the psychological level, we know that long-term well-being depends upon being able to tell your story within a framework of a larger story about your community and the world. And surely that includes an understanding of the meaning of death as well as life. Currently, as a culture, we seem to have a dark imagination populated by the undead—vampires and zombies—and by the living who have literally forgotten their story, as Alzheimer's disease has become one of the greatest fears of my generation.

Is there something the Methodist account of a progressive eschatology has to offer? Only if it is true in the way we understand truth. As Wesleyans, we proceed not from doctrine but from experience guided by the text of scripture and the doctrinal traditions of the historic faith. So the question is whether we can discern the Holy Spirit working among us. Then the task of theology is to name that experience, providing a language and story to revivify our religious imagination.

It is useful to see if we can start from the beginning—reboot the way of salvation. In true Methodist fashion, I offer my own experience as testimony by focusing on the entrance requirement to the Methodist Society. Lester Ruth points out that "when they called for people to 'flee from the wrath to come,' Methodists did not generally have to convince people that God's wrath was coming."[38] As I said earlier, this entrance requirement was the equivalent of an open door because that was the form that spiritual longing took in the religious culture of the time. The presenting symptom of a diseased soul was the experience of guilt for sins and fear of eternal damnation. And we understood that experience to be the work of the Holy Spirit. In the words of "Amazing Grace," incomprehensible for many today, "'Twas grace that taught my heart to fear." It's a bit like the way first-time convicted criminals are scared straight.

Candidly, my experience is that very few people "fear the wrath to come." They do not fear God, and they do not believe in a literal hell. The religious cultural imagination of our time, especially in the Western middle- and upper-class white society, simply doesn't support the images of eternal torment that have been the rhetorical stock-in-trade of many a revival preacher. Those who seek to evangelize in cultures dominated by religions such as Buddhism or Hinduism report the same challenge. In these cultures, the Christian faith finds itself in the position of answering a question people are not asking because they don't share the underlying sentiment. A large number of people we would seek to save are not seeking salvation from sin and death as is understood in the classic theological formulation.

Does that mean prevenient grace is not at work anymore? No; I believe I see the Spirit at work just as intensely as in past ages, but in a different form. We live in a time of great fear, anxiety, and existential hopelessness. Science and technology are offering much but also raising existential questions. Genetic engineering and artificial intelligence are causing us to wonder about the uniqueness of the individual soul and the meaning of human existence. Astronomy and physics are raising fundamental questions about the nature of the universe. Meanwhile, the market economy and the gap between the rich and the poor make billions of people feel, literally, worthless.

I have known great fear in the dark night of my soul, and I sense the same lurking dread in many around me. As a child, I was afraid of Dracula and animals with sharp teeth; as an adult, dementia and the death of a child. But I think the true existential fear of my contemporaries is not of a wrathful God or the consequences of our sins. Our worst fear is that there is no God. It is the nightmarish prospect that there is no meaning in the universe or in our lives. And the consequences at the end of mortal life are not a hot orange and red place out of Dante's *Inferno*. It is the cold black emptiness, the nothingness of deep outer space.

Movies are the primary source of our religious imagination today, and they portray this emptiness. Perhaps the most frightening movie villain in my lifetime is Hannibal Lector in *The Silence of the Lambs*.[39] The chilling essence of his character is not active malice; it is his emptiness of feeling. Indeed, the real-life horrors of our time are the teenaged mass murderers who stare out at us in news coverage with their blank stares. The director of the film *Gravity*,[40] featuring an astronaut trapped in her capsule, called it a "monster movie." But, he said, the monster isn't

71

"gravity"; it is the emptiness of space. The terror was that she would be lost in space. As the story unfolds, she is "found" in a moment of what we could call "prevenient grace" when she cries out to a God she has never prayed to before out of those dark depths. The diseases of emptiness, the absence of meaning and purpose, are the epidemics of drug abuse, depression, and suicide. Certainly, we can see this developing historically in the existential crisis following the illusion-shattering world wars.

There is strong biblical warrant for this understanding of the experience of sin and death. The word *hell* may be translated as "hollow" or dark cave. Matthew speaks of the torment of fire, but he also speaks of it as "outer darkness" (Matthew 22:13 RSV). In Genesis, the time before creation is a world that "was without form and void, and darkness was upon the face of the deep" (Genesis 1:2 RSV). Indeed, sin has always been understood as a condition of being without God, with many of the Psalms and the words of the prophets speaking about the torment of alienation from God.

It is said that "seeing is believing." But it is more the case that believing is a certain way of seeing. Theology is not just a matter of proposing a philosophical framework. Especially for Methodists, theology is an act of naming an experience and, in the naming, helping to enable eyes to see and ears to hear. It is a sacramental process. Wesley would call it a "means of grace."

So perhaps the way to reenchant the Methodist religious imagination and recover a full sense of our progressive eschatological vision is to begin where Wesley began by welcoming others at the point of their real fear—not of wrath and punishment but emptiness and meaninglessness—and then to offer testimony of the love of God and the experience of assurance that comes with knowing Christ and the sense of mission and joy that comes with the cooperative project of the kingdom of God coming "on earth as it is in heaven" (Matthew 6:10 RSV). This is a Methodist way of talking about salvation, to ask both what we are saved *from* and what we are saved *for*.

NOTES

1. See Thomas A. Langford, *Practical Divinity: Theology in the Wesleyan Tradition* (Nashville: Abingdon Press, 1983).

2. "The Nature, Design, and General Rules of the United Societies," in *The Works of the Rev. John Wesley, A.M.*, ed. John Emory, 3rd American Complete and Standard Edition (New York: Carlton & Lanahan, 1831), 5:191.

3. William Shakespeare, *Hamlet*, act 3, scene 1.

4. Wesley, "The Scripture Way of Salvation," in *Works*, 1:384–85.

5. Wesley, "The Way to the Kingdom," in *Works*, 1:64.

6. Ryan Danker, email interview, February 2016.

7. Randy L. Maddox, *Responsible Grace: John Wesley's Practical Theology* (Nashville: Kingswood Books, 1994), 235–39.

8. See Wesley's sermon "The New Creation," in *Works*, 2:82.

9. See Kenneth J. Collins, "Eschatology and Glorification: The Triumph of Holy Love," in *The Theology of John Wesley: Holy Love and the Shape of Grace* (Nashville: Abingdon Press, 2007).

10. Wesley, "The New Creation," in *Works*, 2:87.

11. United Methodist Church, *The United Methodist Hymnal: Book of United Methodist Worship* (Nashville: United Methodist Publishing House, 1989), no. 384.

12. United Methodist Church, *The United Methodist Book of Worship* (Nashville: United Methodist Publishing House, 1992), 721.

13. Wesley, "On Faith," *Works*, 2:388.

14. See Wesley, "On Working Out Our Own Salvation," in *Works*, 2:233–39.

15. See Wesley, "Predestination Calmly Considered," in *Works*, 6:24–60.

16. Wesley, "Of Hell," in *Works*, 2:147–54.

17. Wesley, "On the Resurrection of the Dead," in *Works*, 2:507.

18. Wesley, "On the Resurrection of the Dead," in *Works*, 2:508.

19. See Wesley, "Of Hell," in *Works*, 2:147–54.

20. Wesley, "Of Hell," in *Works*, 2:149.

21. Kenneth J. Collins, *The Theology of John Wesley: Holy Love and the Shape of Grace* (Nashville: Abingdon Press, 2007), 320.

22. Frank Baker, introduction to *Representative Verse of Charles Wesley*, ed. Frank Baker (London: Epworth Press, 1962), xvii.

23. Baker, *Representative Verse of Charles Wesley*, 131.

24. Baker, *Representative Verse of Charles Wesley*, 89.

25. David Hempton, *Methodism: Empire of the Spirit* (New Haven: Yale University Press, 2005), 65; Randy L. Maddox, *Responsible Grace: John Wesley's Practical Theology* (New Haven: Yale University Press, 2005), 68.

26. Kendall Soulen, email interview, February 2016.

27. Kenneth J. Collins, *John Wesley: A Theological Journey* (Nashville: Abingdon Press, 2003), 268.

28. See Hempton, *Methodism*, 30–31.

29. See Lester Ruth, *Early Methodist Life and Spirituality: A Reader* (Nashville: Kingswood Books, 2005).

30. Ruth, *Early Methodist Life and Spirituality*, 142–43.

31. Eileen Guenther, *In Their Own Words: Slave Life and the Power of Spirituals* (St. Louis: MorningStar Music Publishers, 2016).

32. Ruth, *Early Methodist Life and Spirituality*, 143

33. Baker, introduction to *Representative Verse of Charles Wesley*, xvii.

34. United Methodist Church, *The Book of Discipline of the United Methodist Church* (Nashville: United Methodist Publishing House, 1976), 67.

35. See United Methodist Church, *Social Principles of the United Methodist Church, 2013–2016: With Official Text and Teaching Exercises, Plus Our Social Creed* (Nashville: United Methodist Publishing House, 2013).

36. United Methodist Church, *The United Methodist Book of Worship* (Nashville: United Methodist Publishing House, 1992).

37. Ted A. Campbell, *Methodist Doctrine: The Essentials* (Nashville: Abingdon Press, 1999), 82.

38. Ruth, *Early Methodist Life and Spirituality*, 137.

39. *The Silence of the Lambs*, directed by Jonathan Demme (Los Angeles: Orion Pictures, 1991).

40. *Gravity*, directed by Alfonso Cuarzon (Burbank, CA: Warner Brothers, 2013).

Chapter 5

DEATH, RESURRECTION, AND THE TIME IN BETWEEN

A CALVINIST PERSPECTIVE

Richard J. Mouw

Richard J. Mouw, an evangelical scholar, is past president of Fuller Theological Seminary and continues to hold the post of professor of faith and public life.

In 1534 John Calvin, still in his mid-twenties and fairly new to the arena of theological polemics, wrote a treatise in which he passionately attacked some Christian thinkers with whom he disagreed on what he considered a key theological topic. Calvin had only recently left the Catholic Church for the emerging Protestant Reformation movement, but this early tract was directed not against Catholic theologians but against leaders associated with the Anabaptist subgroup within Protestantism. The lengthy title he gave to his essay identifies both the source of his theological concern and the depth of his passion on the subject he is addressing: *Psychopannychia, or, a Refutation of the Error Entertained by Some Unskilful Persons, Who Ignorantly Imagine That in the Interval between Death and the Judgment the Soul Sleeps. Together with an Explanation of the Condition and Life of the Soul after This Present Life.*

Calvin notes that the deniers of a conscious intermediate state between an individual's death and the general resurrection divide into two groups. Some, he says, admit to the reality of a nonphysical human soul but "imagine that it sleeps in *a state of insensibility* from Death to The Judgment-day, when it will awake from its sleep." There are others, he reports, who "will sooner admit anything than its real existence, maintaining that it is merely a vital power which is derived from arterial spirit on the action of the lungs, and being *unable to exist* without body, perishes along with the body, and vanishes away and becomes evanescent till the period when the whole man shall be raised again." Against these denials, Calvin insists "both that it [the soul] is a substance, and after the death of the body [it] truly lives, being endued both with *sense and understanding*."[1] In making his case, he amasses many biblical passages, offering extensive commentaries upon them.

Twenty-five years later, when Calvin published the final edition of his classic *Institutes of the Christian Religion*, his treatment of that subject was more subdued. Perhaps he tempered his rhetoric upon becoming aware in the intervening decades that Martin Luther—certainly not numbered among the "unskilful persons" who had earlier so provoked Calvin—had endorsed the soul-sleep position. The German reformer had proclaimed in a sermon: "We shall suddenly rise on the last day, without knowing how we have come into death and through death. We shall sleep, until He comes and knocks on the little grave and says, 'Doctor Martin, get up!' Then I shall rise in a moment, and be with him forever.'"[2]

Whatever caused Calvin to modify his tone on the subject, he now focused in his discussion of the afterlife much more on the resurrection of the body. All who want to "receive the fruits of Christ's benefits," he said, must "raise their minds to the resurrection."[3] And given that as our primary focus, he argued, "it is neither lawful nor expedient to inquire too curiously concerning our souls' intermediate state" since "it is foolish and rash to inquire concerning unknown matters more deeply than God permits us to know. Scripture goes no further than to say that Christ is present with them, and receives them into paradise that they may obtain consolation, while the souls of the reprobate suffer such torments as they deserve."[4]

Calvin's comments may be more muted here than they were twenty-five years earlier, but he had not backed off from his affirmation that the intermediate state is one of a continuing consciousness. In that state the redeemed experience "consolation," while the unredeemed are in a condition of suffering.

CONTINUED CONSCIOUSNESS

The question of continued consciousness in the intermediate state is much debated these days by theologians and Christian philosophers. One important factor in this present interest in the topic is a strong reaction that has been taking place against Platonistic metaphysics in theological circles during the past half century. Much of this has been stimulated by the emphases associated with the biblical theology movement that emerged in Europe during the years following World War II, where a new critical attention was given to the philosophical assumptions that had long been influential in Christian theology. Similar sensitivities were at work in the *aggiornamento*, the theological updating that occurred as a result of the Catholic Church's Second Vatican Council.

A prominent feature of this critical attention has been the attempt to "de-Platonize" Christian theology, especially regarding the theological understanding of the nature and calling of humans. Much damage had been done, it has been argued, by the Greek dualism wherein a human being was seen to be a composite of two different kinds of substances: a rational-spiritual soul and a physical body, with the nonphysical component of our shared nature being higher—closer to God—than the corporeal aspects of our nature. At its worst, Christian theology had borrowed heavily from the Platonistic notion that the body is the prison house of the soul and that death is a release of human souls from their present state of bondage.

OSCAR CULLMANN'S PERSPECTIVE

The contrast between the Platonistic viewpoint and biblical teaching was sketched out compellingly by the Swiss theologian Oscar Cullmann, one of the leaders of the biblical theology movement. Cullman began his influential essay on the themes of immortality and resurrection by comparing the deaths of Socrates and Jesus.[5] Having been sentenced to death, Socrates engages in a calm philosophical discussion with friends who are visiting him in his prison cell. When the conversation is over, Socrates sips the poisonous hemlock, expressing cheerful anticipation of the separation of his soul from his body. Jesus, on the other hand, sweats drops of blood in the Garden of Gethsemane as he pleads with the Father to allow the cup of suffering to pass from him. Later, as he hangs dying on the cross at Calvary, he cries out in agony over his experience of abandonment.[6]

What is clearly on display here, says Cullmann, is the contrast between two radically differing conceptions of the meaning of death. For Socrates, death is the welcome release of the spiritual from the physical. For Jesus, death is an enemy that destroys and threatens the destruction of the whole person. Cullmann explores the underlying theological issues here by giving careful attention to anthropological data of the New Testament. In doing so, he allows for a kind of duality that the biblical writers attribute to human beings, albeit not that of a radically separable soul and body. While the words "soul" and "body" do appear frequently in the Bible, he argues, the real contrast for Paul and others is between "the inner" and "the outer" person. Our inner and outer lives need each other, since "both are created by God." Our inner lives require a home in a body. While this inner life "can, to be sure, somehow lead a shady existence without the body, like the dead in Sheol according to the Old Testament," this shadowy existence is not really "a *genuine life*."[7]

Having offered this portrayal, Cullmann celebrates the doctrine of the resurrection of the body as the central teaching regarding postmortem survival. But he does not hold back from offering a nuanced account regarding the nature of the intermediate state. He observes that in 2 Corinthians 5:1–10 the Apostle Paul expresses anxiety over the "nakedness" of an interim condition when he is no longer in the body but not yet resurrected. But in this same passage, having expressed his "natural anxiety" over the very real threat posed by the destruction of the body, Paul also voices much confidence that he will experience "Christ's proximity, *even in this interim state.*" The inner person is not abandoned by the Holy Spirit when the outer person disappears.[8] Cullmann is willing to live with the metaphysical implications of his insistence on a continuing consciousness of the disembodied inner person. He strongly criticizes Barth, for example, for using the sleep metaphor as grounds for insisting that a person does not experience the passage of time between death and resurrection. Those who are "dead in Christ" do experience some sort of state of consciousness prior to the resurrection, Cullmann argues. They "are still in time; they, too, are waiting. 'How long, oh Lord?' cry the martyrs who are sleeping under the altar in John's Apocalypse ([Revelation] 6:11)."[9]

In a helpful way, Cullmann speaks directly to the metaphysical implications of what he is allowing for here. It is fair to ask, he says, "whether in this fashion we have not been led again, in the last analysis, to the Greek doctrine of immortality." And the fact is, he continues,

> There is a sense in which a kind of *approximation* to the Greek teaching does actually take place, to the extent that the inner man, who has already been transformed by the Spirit (Romans 6:3ff) and consequently made alive, continues to live with Christ in this transformed state, in the condition of sleep. . . . Here we observe at least a certain analogy to the "immortality of the soul," but the distinction remains nonetheless radical.

To be sure, Cullmann insists, some key differences between the biblical and the Greek views remain. Death is indeed an enemy for the Christian. The fact of a residual consciousness for the human person after dying is not due to anything about "the natural essence of the soul." The interim state is, for the believer, a "waiting for the resurrection."[10]

It is important to note explicitly here that all that Cullmann says on this subject applies exclusively to the Christian believer. He tells us nothing about the postmortem prospects of human beings in general. Indeed, he even stipulates that the Christian who has died enters into this sleep state through "a divine intervention from outside, through the Holy Spirit, who must already have quickened the inner man in earthly life by His miraculous power."[11] This too reinforces his insistence that there is considerable distance between the New Testament perspective and the Greek doctrine of immortality. Of course, it could be that God performs a somewhat different kind of miracle for those who die without having been transformed in their inner beings by the Spirit, perhaps sustaining in them a *fearful* waiting for the resurrection. But that is not a topic that Cullman discusses.

N. T. WRIGHT'S POSITION

More recently, N. T. Wright does address the postmortem condition of both believer and unbeliever in his own nuanced discussion of these same issues. Wright speaks to that specific area of concern only after elaborating at length on the need for hope—or, to borrow a phrase from the subtitle of his best-selling book on resurrection, "rethinking heaven." In looking at what requires this rethinking, Wright continues the theological campaign against Hellenistic philosophical influences, with Plato playing a villain role of sorts. In contrast to the Pauline teaching that our *bodies* will "put on immortality" (1 Corinthians 15:53), past theologians have too often taught, says Wright, that we can look forward to a "*disembodied* immortality," a perspective heavily influenced by the Platonistic insistence that "all human beings have an immortal element within them, normally referred to as soul."[12]

Like Cullmann, however, Wright does not deny a conscious state of "being with Christ" between a person's death and the final resurrection. This state is, he says, one "in which the dead are held firmly within the conscious love of God and the conscious presence of Jesus Christ while they await that day."[13] What Wright wants us to be clear about in all of this, however, "is that heaven and hell are not, so to speak, what the whole game is about. . . . The major, central, framing question is that of God's purpose of rescue and recreation for the whole world, the entire cosmos. The destiny of the individual human beings must be understood within that context."[14]

Having given some attention to the condition of those who, having died, enter into a conscious state of "being with the Lord," Wright also directly addresses the state of the unredeemed after their individual deaths and prior to the general resurrection. Wright is no universalist. other "I find it quite impossible . . . to suppose that there will be no ultimate condemnation, no final loss, no human beings to whom, as C. S. Lewis put it, God will eventually say, '*Thy* will be done.'" Those who have openly rejected God's redeeming purposes will have, Wright says, so dehumanized themselves so as to fatally damage the image of God in which they were created. Thus, "with the death of the body in which they inhabited God's good world, in which the flickering flame of goodness had not been completely snuffed out, they pass simultaneously not only beyond hope but also beyond pity," as they "still exist in an ex-human state, no longer reflecting their maker in any meaningful sense."[15]

HIGHER/LOWER DUALISM

Given that my overall purpose here is to discuss John Calvin's views on the afterlife, why go into these details of the cases made by both Cullmann and Wright regarding a conscious intermediate state? Full disclosure in answering this question: as one who identifies with the Calvinist tradition, I have a strong interest in presenting Calvin's general perspective on theological matters and his views on "last things" in particular in the most favorable manner that I can manage. And this is out of respect not only for the convictions Calvin expressed in his sixteenth-century context but also for the ways those convictions provide help for addressing contemporary concerns.

Anyone who wants to highlight the strengths of Calvin's views for contemporary theological exploration, however, must at the same time admit some weaknesses in his theology. And there is at least one weakness in the way in which a regrettable influence of Plato seems to be at work in Calvin's view of human nature.

In assessing Plato's dualistic understanding of the human person, it is important to keep a distinction in mind between his dualistic understanding of the basic composition of a human being, on the one hand, and what we might think of as Plato's ranking in making his distinction between soul and body on the other. When Cullmann says that the Apostle Paul's affirmations regarding the intermediate state can be rightly seen "as a kind of *approximation* to the Greek teaching," Cullmann is implicitly endorsing a metaphysical view concerning the *composition* of the human person. We are the kinds of beings whose full natures cannot be understood in purely physical terms. We are more than mere bodies. There is something in us that can continue to be conscious when the body goes into the grave. Calvin would agree with that. If someone wants to see that as compatible with at least a modest version of Plato's compositional dualism, so be it.

But this compositional account in Plato's thought was intimately linked to a higher/lower dualism. The soul, in Platonism, is intrinsically immortal, belonging to the unchanging realm of noncorporeal Forms. The body is of a lower reality, and it inhibits the soul from focusing on eternal things. And the influence of this ranking element in Plato's thought does show up in Calvin's writings, as when he insists that "when Christ commended his spirit to the Father and Stephen to his Christ, they meant only that when the spirit is freed from the prison house of the body, God is its perpetual guardian" and that "we journey away from God so long as we dwell in the flesh, but that we enjoy his presence outside the flesh."[16]

This is where we have much to learn from the insistence by many recent theologians that this biblical viewpoint leads to a very different understanding of our present lives as believers. The distinction between spiritual and physical activities and dispositions is to be understood not in terms of two different substances but rather as pointing to the basic patterns with which we direct our lives. To put it in blunt terms, marital physical intimacy can for believing couples be spiritual, whereas a prideful praying for God to curse those with whom one disagrees can be fleshly.

It is significant that when Calvin gives expression to this higher/lower dualism, he typically does not make any reference in that context to the resurrected state. But when he does emphasize the resurrection as the glorious hope for which the souls of the departed Saints are yearning, his views comport quite clearly with the sort of perspective on the Christian life set forth by, say, an N. T. Wright.

THE INFLUENCE OF SCIENTIFIC ADVANCES

The composition question in relationship to the afterlife is getting much attention these days, in good part because of groundbreaking work done in recent decades in the scientific study of the brain and its role in affecting behaviors, thoughts, and emotions. The issues raised by these scientific advances have stimulated much philosophical discussion about what the relationship is between brain states and what we ordinarily classify as states of consciousness. What is the relationship between a thought I am having about a slice of pepperoni pizza and the neural processes occurring in my brain when I am having that thought. Does the brain event *accompany* the mental event? Or is the mental event in some important sense *identical with* the brain event? Is our ordinary talk about brain and mind as two separate things really about only one thing: using two modes of discourse, consciousness talk and brain talk, that in fact refer to one "stuff"?

Those are big and complex metaphysical topics, and I do not intend to address them here. But I do want at least to acknowledge that the recent theological debates about the afterlife have occurred in a broader intellectual climate in which new scientific concerns have created some of the sense of urgency in the debates and fostered a spirit of theological caution in moving too quickly from the biblical data compositional affirmations. The Dutch Reformed theologian Berkouwer addressed this issue in observing that that any attempt to single out specific biblical terms for human parts (spirit, flesh, body, or heart) in exploring compositional issues will inevitably run into much messiness. The biblical writers, he says, use such terms "in very concrete and extremely varied ways." The Bible's overall intent, then, is not so much "to reveal to us something of the composition of man" but rather "to speak of man as a whole."[17]

This not to say, though, that the biblical references are simply irrelevant to questions of composition. There is still room for looking for at least some biblical guidance on the composition topic. Berkouwer himself admits as much. He notes that divine "revelation directs our glance toward man in his totality, in his relation to God." Berkouwer does allow for the fact that while the Bible's intent is not "to reveal to us something of the composition of man,"[18] it does "incidentally" point to certain compositional realities along the way.[19]

I find this suggestion helpful, in that it gives us permission to explore, albeit with due caution, questions of this sort: What kind of metaphysical entity must a human person *be* to be capable of the kinds of things the Bible says about us? Given that we cannot get a lot of metaphysical mileage from the Bible's unsystematic references to spirit or heart or soul, can we at least discern what kinds of beings we must be, in metaphysical terms, for the Bible to say what it means to say when using these terms?

The intermediate state topic is especially poignant in this regard. When the Apostle Paul celebrates the fact that when he is "absent from the body" he is "present with the Lord," what compositional account of human nature best comports with his confident claim?

A PERSONAL REFLECTION

During the seventeen years I served as a faculty member at Calvin College, I regularly taught introductory philosophy courses. When I moved in 1985 to Fuller Theological Seminary, a graduate-level school, that kind of teaching was no longer a part of my assignment. Every once in a while, though, I have occasion to look into my file of lecture notes for those introductory courses, and I have been reminded how I would exposit at length Socrates's view, as reported in Plato's *Phaedo*, of the afterlife as a state of being where the soul passively contemplates the eternal Forms, and then I would explain to my students what I took to be the biblical view. "The Bible depicts the future life as a resurrected state," I would tell my students. "And that means that we will actively reign with Christ in that glorious kingdom in which all things have been made new." To reinforce my point, I would say things like this: "Heaven for us will be *doing* things. We will continue to solve problems and take on challenges. And we will go about our active service of God without being plagued anymore by the realities of sin."

I think N. T. Wright would have been pleased with those lectures. They comported well with his advocacy for a robust conception of the resurrected life as active participation in the fullness of the kingdom of Christ, where all things will be renewed.

Though I continue to endorse that robust view of things theologically, I confess that while reading my earlier class notes and studying the views of Wright and others about the coming kingdom, the notion of such a busy Christian afterlife makes me tired. The idea of being active for all eternity is much less appealing to me now than it was in my younger days. I would even settle for a millennium or so of passively contemplating Platonic Forms!

This shift in my eschatological mood—if not my theological convictions—obviously has something to do with a change in my personal life situation. We should not be surprised that the sorts of eschatological expectations that attract us in our youth would differ from those that give us comfort in our later years.

The personal tension that I have just described corresponds to a distinction some scholars have set forth between anthropocentric and theocentric perspectives on the afterlife. As Colleen McDannell and Bernhard Lang have employed the distinction, in theocentric accounts the souls of the dead in heaven experience a beatific union with God, even to the point that their memories of previous experiences are lost; whereas in anthropocentric conceptions the sense of identity is an extension of the previous earthly existence, and the preoccupations of heaven are not unlike those that presently occupy us.[20]

Those perspectives, then, that focus on intrahuman relations and activities—reunion with loved ones, life in "the Peaceable Kingdom," the perfect actualization of justice for the oppressed, and so on—stand in contrast to those that focus exclusively on, say, "being with Jesus," or the *visio dei*.

But we do not have to see the two conceptions in either-or terms. Carol Zaleski has rightly insisted that rather than having to choose for one or the other, "a more adequate perspective would be theocentric and anthropocentric at once." To illustrate, she cites an account of heaven she found in a story from tenth-century Ireland where the visionary "'discovers that the saints who encircle the throne have acquired the power to face in all directions at once'—'a scene that captures the sociability of the beatific vision.'"[21]

John Calvin certainly did not see the need to choose between the theocentric and the anthropocentric. He observes that while for the redeemed it is a blessed hope to know "that the kingdom of God will be fulfilled with splendor, joy, happiness, and glory," it is even more blessed to know that when "that day comes . . . he will reveal to us his glory, that we may behold it face to face."[22]

BECOMING LIKE GOD?

Since I am offering these Calvinist comments about the afterlife at the invitation of a great intellectual center of the Latter-day Saints, I will not resist the temptation here to say something about the relevance of the theocentric-anthropocentric distinction for Latter-day Saint eschatology. Many members of other faiths see the Latter-day Saint understanding of the afterlife as dominated almost exclusively by anthropocentric themes, as in the vision of families living happily in a future paradise. Nor is that strong emphasis on the horizontal-relational dimensions of the Latter-day Saint conception of life in the celestial kingdom a mere expression of "folk Mormonism." It flows naturally from the Latter-day Saint theological insistence, rooted in the acceptance of extrabiblical deliverances attributed to continuing revelations, of the eternality of family and marriage.

Just as I do not want to purge my own Calvinist eschatological perspective of all anthropological elements, I also have no desire to urge that kind of purging for the Latter-day Saint vision of the afterlife. The theocentric is clearly a central emphasis in the view of our present pilgrimages as believers. Robert Millet makes that very clear in his insistence that for Latter-day Saint teaching at its best the path to deification is possible only "through the cleansing and transforming power of the blood of Jesus Christ."[23] If the full realization of the process of becoming godlike has to be seen as the culmination of what is already occurring in our present lives, then the crucial theocentric dimensions of the way of holiness will certainly extend into eternity. Thus Millet's appeal to the words of Joseph Smith on our never-ending reliance and dependence on divine favor: our goal of becoming "heirs of God, and joint heirs with Jesus Christ," the prophet insisted, is possible only "through the love of the Father, the mediation of Jesus Christ, and the gift of the Holy Spirit."[24]

Those affirmations are unqualifiedly theocentric in a way that evokes gratitude in my Calvinist heart. The distinctive emphasis of the Calvinist branch of Reformation thought is the way that God's sovereign grace reaches into our deep places, bringing about a transforming spiritual renewal that we could never achieve by our own efforts as sinners. And the terminology employed in Robert Millet's citation of Joseph Smith on our eternal destiny comports well, to my spiritual ears, with that Calvinist emphasis. We are everlastingly dependent on the realities of the Father's love, the Son's mediatorial redemptive work, and the gift of the Holy Spirit's sustaining power.

For my twenty-first century appropriation of Calvinist thought, these realities—the gracious operations of the three members of the Godhead—define the essential infrastructure of everlasting life. Whatever our understanding of the metaphysics of what we refer to as the human "soul," our hope for the future, both in our present lives and in what will happen us after we walk through the valley of the shadow of death, is grounded firmly in the gracious promise—a biblical promise that I have heard my Latter-day Saint friends quote frequently—that while we are already sons and daughters of the living God: "it doth not yet appear what we shall be," and when the Savior appears "we shall be like him; for we shall see him as he is" (1 John 3:2).

NOTES

1. John Calvin, *Psychopannychia*, in *Tracts and Treatises in Defense of the Reformed Faith*, trans. Henry Beveridge (Grand Rapids, MI: Eerdmans, 1958), 3:419–20.

2. Quoted by T. A. Kantonen, *The Christian Hope* (Philadelphia: United Lutheran Church in America, Board of Publication, 1954), 37.

3. John Calvin, *Institutes of the Christian Religion*, ed. John T. McNeill, trans. Ford Lewis Battles (Philadelphia: Westminster Press, 1960), 3.25.2, 989.

4. Calvin, *Institutes*, 3.25.6, 997.

5. I explore Cullmann's views on this subject, along with the more general relationship between philosophical conceptions of human nature and biblical thought, at greater length in my essay "Imago Dei and Philosophical Anthropology," *Christian Scholar's Review* 40, no. 3 (Spring 2012): 253–66.

6. Oscar Cullmann, "Immortality of the Soul or Resurrection of the Dead: The Witness of the New Testament," reprinted in *Immortality*, ed. Terence Penelhum (Belmont, CA: Wadsworth, 1973), 60–63.

7. Cullmann, "Immortality," 69.

8. Cullmann, "Immortality," 81.

9. Cullmann, "Immortality," 79.

10. Cullmann, "Immortality," 83.

11. Cullmann, "Immortality," 83.

12. N. T. Wright, *Surprised by Hope: Rethinking Heaven, the Resurrection, and the Mission of the Church* (New York: Harper One, 2008), 160.

13. Wright, *Surprised by Hope*, 172.

14. Wright, *Surprised by Hope*, 184.

15. Wright, *Surprised by Hope*, 182–83.

16. Calvin, *Institutes*, 1.15.2, 184, 186.

17. G. C. Berkouwer, *Studies in Dogmatics: Man: The Image of God* (Grand Rapids, MI: Eerdmans, 1962), 199.

18. Berkouwer, *Image*, 199.

19. Berkouwer, *Image*, 203.

20. Colleen McDannell and Bernhard Lang, *Heaven: A History* (New Haven: Yale University Press, 1988).

21. Carol Zaleski, "Fear of Heaven," *Christian Century*, 14 March 2001.

22. Calvin, *Institutes*, 3.25.10, 1004–5.

23. Robert L. Millet, *Modern Mormonism: Myths and Realities* (Salt Lake City: Greg Kofford Books, 2010), 89.

24. Joseph Smith, *Lectures on Faith* (Salt Lake City: Deseret Book, 1985), 5:3, quoted in Millet, *Modern Mormonism*, 89.

Chapter 6

THE NEAR-DEATH EXPERIENCE

WHY LATTER-DAY SAINTS ARE SO INTERESTED

Brent L. Top

Brent L. Top, a Latter-day Saint scholar, is a professor of Church history and doctrine at Brigham Young University.

First published in 1975, the book *Life After Life* by Dr. Raymond A. Moody has sold over thirteen million copies worldwide. In this landmark book, Moody coined a new term to describe the phenomenon he had repeatedly encountered in his medical practice. The term *near-death experience* (NDE) is widely used today—both for good and for ill—depending on how a person views it. Subsequent books by Dr. Moody, such as *Reflections on Life After Life*, *The Light Beyond*, *Glimpses of Eternity*, and *Coming Back*, further examined dimensions of the near-death experience. More than seven million additional copies of these books were sold. Moody's work opened the publishing floodgates. Over the next forty-plus years have come hundreds of books, articles, documentaries, and even Hollywood movies on the subject. Moody and the study of near-death experiences that he founded are not without their critics, however. Criticism, concern, dismissal, and denunciation have also surrounded this work, coming both from secular and religious circles. Dr. Elisabeth Kubler-Ross, whose groundbreaking book *On Death and Dying* was influential in the development of hospice services for the terminally ill, predicted such a reaction in the foreword she penned for Moody's *Life After Life*. "Dr. Moody will have to be prepared for a lot of criticism, mainly from two areas," Kubler-Ross wrote.

> There will be members of the clergy who will be upset by anyone who dares to do research in an area which is supposed to be taboo. Some religious representatives of a denominational church have already expressed their criticism of studies like this. One priest referred to it as "selling cheap grace." Others simply [feel] that the question of life after death should remain an issue of blind faith and should not be questioned by anyone. The second group of people that Dr. Moody can expect to respond to his book with concern are scientists and physicians who regard this kind of study as "unscientific."[1]

Although there was the expected criticism and suspicion, it can be argued that Moody's books and the works of many other NDE researchers and experiencers have, to date, received greater acceptance among Latter-day Saints proportionally than those of other Christian faith traditions. Why are Latter-day Saints so interested in near-death experiences? What does The Church of Jesus Christ of Latter-day Saints bring to the discussion? In my estimation, the answers to these questions are found in our *doctrine* and *history*. Let me illustrate how these two factors are intertwined in our beliefs regarding the afterlife and our reactions to modern research and reports of near-death experiences.

Shortly after the release of his book, *Life After Life*, Raymond Moody visited Salt Lake City as part of a publicity tour promoting the book. He was interviewed by the local media. One radio interview in particular highlighted the keen interest of the Latter-day Saint community in his topic. It was with the Church-owned radio station KSL, a 50,000-watt station whose broadcast signal could be received throughout the Intermountain West and beyond. What stood out to me from the program were the many comments and questions that came from the listening audience during the call-in portion of the program. Predictably, most were Latter-day Saints who asked Dr. Moody these "golden questions": "How much do you know about The Church of Jesus Christ of Latter-day Saints?" and "Would you like to know more?" Interestingly, that very month an article appeared in the *Ensign*, the Church's official magazine, entitled "The Spirit World, Our Next Home." Many of the radio listeners asked Dr. Moody if they could send him a copy. "I think I have already had about a hundred sent to me," quipped Moody. Whether he knew it before that radio program or publishing his classic work, he knew it then—Latter-day Saints are keenly interested in what an ancient Book of Mormon prophet called "the state of the soul between death and the resurrection" (Alma 40:11). It has been so from the Church's very formation.

Speaking in honor of his recently deceased friend, Joseph Smith Jr. declared in Nauvoo, Illinois, on 9 October 1843:

> All men know that all men must die.— What is the object of our coming into existence. then dying and falling away to be here no more? This is a subject we ought to study more than any other, which we ought to study day and night.— If we have claim on our heavenly father for any thing it is for knowledge on this important subject— could we read and comprehend all that has been writtn from the days of Adam on the relation of man to God & angels. and the spirits of Just men in a future state. we should know very little about it. could you gaze in heaven 5 minute. you would know more— than you possibly would can know by read[ing] all that ever was writtn on the subject.[2]

Recognizing, as the Prophet taught, that Heavenly Father has revealed "much knowledge on this important subject," the doctrinal teachings as found both in canonical revelations and authoritative sermons of Church leaders are rich with insights into life beyond the grave. This knowledge, Latter-day Saints believe, not only gives us a glimpse past the doorway of death into eternity but also yields important perspective into the purposes of life. Thus, the study of death and the afterlife is both faith affirming and life enriching. Explaining why he personally (as well as others of the leaders of the Church) spoke so frequently on this "important subject," Elder Orson Pratt, a nineteenth-century Church Apostle and one of the Church's greatest theologians, stated:

> And do not forget to look forward to the joys ahead, if we do [forget], we will become careless, dormant, and sluggish, and we will think we do not see much ahead to be anticipated, but if we keep our minds upon the prize that lays ahead—upon the vast fields of knowledge to be poured out upon the righteous, and the glories that are to be revealed, and the heavenly things in the future state, we shall be continually upon the alert. . . . Let these things sink down in our minds continually, and they will make us joyful, and careful to do unto our neighbors as we would they should do unto us. Lest we should come short of some of these things is the reason I have [often] touched upon the future state of man . . . to stir up the pure minds of the Saints that we may prepare for the things that are not far ahead, and let all the actions of our lives have a bearing in relation to the future.[3]

These statements clearly illustrate how both our *doctrine* and *history* combine to create a fertile seedbed for our interest in near-death experiences and other accounts of what some may call "divine encounters" with life after death. Arguably, Latter-day Saints in the last several decades may have demonstrated more positive interest and acceptance of these things than adherents to Christian traditions. The side effects of such keen interest may be both positive and negative. Positive effects can include affirmation of one's beliefs, deeper understanding of what lies beyond this life, comfort when a loved one dies, hope of a heavenly reunion with family and friends, deeper insight into the purposes of life, and greater love for and desire to accept God's will. However, the downside or potentially dangerous side effects may include distortion of or distraction from the word of God and sound doctrinal teachings, false feelings of spiritual security, and even apostasy. So, for Latter-day

Saints, at least (and I assume for other Christians as well), interest in all things "beyond the grave" must also be tempered with some cautions and safeguards. With that said, let us now examine some Latter-day Saint doctrine and history that may serve as a basis for the intense interest for the near-death experience phenomenon. I'll conclude with some words of caution and conviction.

DOCTRINE

Since Raymond Moody first coined the term *near-death experience*, numerous other scientists and scholars have studied the phenomenon and have identified core elements of NDEs. Although each NDE is unique, some of the common characteristics include:

- Lifting out of one's body and being able to observe other people, events, and activities going on (e.g., resuscitative efforts)
- Intense emotions: commonly of profound peace, well-being, and love
- Rapid movement through darkness, often toward an indescribable light—becoming "engulfed" in the Being of Light's overwhelming love and knowledge
- A sense of being somewhere else, like a spiritual realm or world
- Incredibly rapid, sharp thinking and observations, enhanced senses and abilities
- Encounter with deceased loved ones, sacred figures, or unrecognized beings with whom communication is mind-to-mind
- A life review, reliving actions and feeling their emotional impact on others
- A flood of knowledge about life and the nature of the universe
- Sometimes a decision to return to the body

These core elements feel familiar to most Latter-day Saints because of unique teachings regarding the immortal human soul, the nature and capacities of the spirit body, and the purposes and conditions of the postearth spirit realm. There are many other doctrinal teachings—both authoritative and quasi-authoritative—that may be seen by Latter-day Saints as interesting similarities to or even important explanations of near-death experiences. There are many books in the literature (some I have even authored) that do just that, but for the purpose of this paper, I will briefly examine three doctrines—the immortality of the soul, the spirit body, and the purposes and conditions of the spirit world.

IMMORTALITY OF THE SOUL

The canonical work known as the Doctrine and Covenants contains doctrine that Latter-day Saints believe came to Joseph Smith through revelation from God. In one section, we read that "man was also in the beginning with God [meaning before the world was created]. Intelligence, or the light of truth, was not created or made, neither indeed can be. . . . For man is spirit. The elements are eternal" (Doctrine and Covenants 93:29, 33).

In another canonical work known as the Pearl of Great Price, in the Book of Abraham, a vision of Abraham is recorded that likewise speaks of the eternal nature of man: "Now the Lord had shown unto me, Abraham, the intelligences that were organized before the world was; and among all these there were many of the noble and great ones. . . . [God] stood among those that were spirits, and he saw that they were good; and he said unto me: Abraham, thou art one of them; thou wast chosen before thou wast born" (Abraham 3:22–23).

Elaborating upon this doctrinal foundation, Joseph Smith taught in 1844 that "the Spirit of Man . . . existed from Eternity and will exist to eternity.[4] A generation later in 1909, the First Presidency of the Church authoritatively redeclared the doctrine of the Church that "all men existed in spirit before any man existed in the flesh."[5]

Thus, Latter-day Saints believe that each of us lived as spirit beings before we were ever born into this world. Without an understanding of the doctrine of man's premortal existence as spirits, it is virtually impossible to understand beliefs concerning the afterlife and the nature of spirits and the spirit world.

SPIRIT BODY

The Doctrine and Covenants declares that the "spirit of man [is] in the likeness of his person" (Doctrine and Covenants 77:2). Similarly, we read in the previously cited 1909 First Presidency doctrinal declaration that the earthly body "is only the clothing of the spirit" and that "the spirit of man is in the form of man."[6] There is a familiar object lesson taught that illustrates this doctrine. President Boyd K. Packer explained how the physical body is the tabernacle for the immortal spirit by comparing it to a glove and the spirit to a hand. The glove covers the hand, but the hand is the real living part. Death is like taking off the glove.[7] Brigham Young, prophetic successor to Joseph Smith likewise taught that if a person were to "take the spirit from the body, the body is lifeless."[8]

Because of Latter-day Saint teaching that our spirits are immortal, having lived with God before being clothed with a physical body at birth, Church members understand that a spirit body, with all its unique features and capacities, continues to live even after the physical body dies. Perhaps we Latter-day Saints take this doctrine for granted. For many near-death experiencers of other faiths, it comes as a great surprise that at their death they still had a body of some sort. No wonder Latter-day Saints feel a sense of spiritual kinship to those who report experiences such as these:

- "To my surprise," one experiencer reported, "I found that I still had hands, and feet, and a body, for I had always regarded the souls as a something without shape and void.

. . . To find, that though I was dead I still had form was new to me."[9]

- An eighteenth-century man who had what could be could called an encounter with the afterlife wrote: "On the basis of all my experience . . . I can insist that [spirits] are completely people in form. They do have faces, eyes, ears, chests, arms, hands, and feet. They do see each other, hear each other, and talk with each other. In short, nothing proper to man whatever is missing, except they are not clothed with a material body."[10]

- Dr. George Ritchie in his classic near-death experience account recorded in *Return from Tomorrow*, expressed shock that he could actually see his dead body lying on the bed he had just left. "I was me, wide awake, only without a physical body to function in," Ritchie reported.[11]

- Dr. Raymond Moody reported that many of the NDErs he studied reported they had a body of some sort that "mimicked the contours of their physical form."

- Based on her years of hearing the near-death experiences of those with whom she worked, Elizabeth Kubler-Ross concluded that the spiritual body is an exact replica of the physical body, "lacking only its defects."[12]

That the spirit body lacks the defects, deterioration, and deficiencies common to the earthly body is also fundamental in Latter-day Saint doctrine. Brigham Young spoke of the physical body as being a "coarser organization" in comparison to the perfect spirit body.[13] "It [the spirit] is not encumbered with this clog of dirt we are carrying around here so that when we advance in years we have to be stubbing along and be careful lest we fall down. . . . But yonder, how different! . . . Here we are continually troubled with ills and ailments of various kinds, . . . but in the spirit world we are free from all this and enjoy life, glory, and intelligence."[14] To Latter-day Saints, it is a comforting doctrine to know that the physical limitations will fall away, that disease and sickness in the spirit world are nonexistent, and that aging and handicaps are nowhere to be found. To many members, much of modern near-death research is fascinating, not because it teaches anything new doctrinally about the spirit world but because it confirms those truths that they accept as revelations from God. A couple of examples illustrate this:

- Dr. Elizabeth Kubler-Ross observed that terminally ill patients who had near-death experiences reported that their spirit bodies were healthy and strong. "Quadriplegics are no longer paralyzed," she wrote, "multiple sclerosis patients who have been in wheelchairs for years say that when they were out of their bodies, they were able to sing and dance."[15]

- Dr. Kenneth Ring, one of the world's foremost near-death experience researchers (who is not a Latter-day Saint) conducted a groundbreaking study of people who had been born blind—never having had any vision whatsoever—who had near-death experiences and reported being able to clearly see. Though they never had seen colors or light or anything before in their lives, they described in detail people, colors, scenes, and so forth, they saw in the spirit realm.[16]

- A man who lost a large portion of his leg in an accident saw, in his out-of-body experience, the doctors working on his maimed body. He said, "I could feel my [spirit] body, and it was whole. . . . I felt that all of me was there."[17]

Because of the long-held doctrine of the spirit body, these kinds of NDE experiences make perfect sense to Latter-day Saints, even though they may leave some medical doctors and scientists scratching their heads.

In addition to the perfection of the spirit body, Latter-day Saints believe that once freed from the limitations of the physical body, spirits have enhanced capacities and powers relating to communication, movement, and activities. From the Doctrine and Covenants, Church members learn that "all spirit is matter, but it is more fine and pure, and can only be discerned by purer eyes" (Doctrine and Covenants 131:7). The refined, pure nature of spirit matter affects how the spirit moves about, communicates, learns, and comprehends. Within the doctrinal teachings of Church Apostles, numerous statements about this can be found. Joseph Smith, Brigham Young, and the Pratt brothers—Orson and Parley, two of the great Latter-day Saint theological minds—repeatedly taught of the remarkable powers possessed by the departed righteous while in the spirit world. Joseph Smith taught that the spirits of the faithful possessing a portion of God's infinite power are "enveloped in flaming fire"— fire representing God's glory and power.[18]

THE SPIRIT WORLD

The Book of Mormon provides Latter-day Saints with direct teaching regarding life after death. The ancient prophet Alma recorded that "there is a space between the time of death and the resurrection" (Alma 40:9). Expounding upon that doctrine, Alma explained that he learned from an angel concerning the "state of the soul between death and the resurrection." He recorded:

> Behold, it has been made known unto me . . . that the spirits of all men, as soon as they are departed from this mortal body, yea, the spirits of all men, whether they be good or evil, are taken home to that God who gave them life.
>
> And then shall it come to pass, that the spirits of those who are righteous are received into a state of happiness, which is called paradise, a state of rest, a state of peace, where they shall rest from all their troubles and from all care, and sorrow. (Alma 40:11–12)

In stark contrast to the blessed state of the faithful who enter into a paradise at death, Alma explained that the wicked—those who in life "chose evil works rather than good"—are in "darkness, and a state of awful, fearful looking" forward to the "wrath of God" that will ultimately befall them. "Thus they remain in this state," Alma declared, "as well as the righteous in paradise until the time of their resurrection" (Alma 40:13–14).

Latter-day Saints accept subsequent revelations and teachings of latter-day prophets and apostles within the Church that amplify Book of Mormon teachings on the world of spirits who are righteous, wicked, and everything in between. From latter-day prophets and apostles, members learn that the primary purpose for the spirit world is continued progression and preparation for the resurrection—all humankind being given a full opportunity to accept the Lord and his gospel. Shortly before his death in 1844, Joseph Smith taught the Latter-day Saints that "all those [who] die in the faith go to the prison of spirits to preach to the dead . . . that they may live according to God in the spirit . . . and [be made] happy by these means."[19] On another occasion, the Prophet taught that knowledge of Christ and his gospel "saves a man, and in the world of spirits a man cannot be exalted but by [this] knowledge; so long as a man will not give heed to the commandments, he must abide without salvation."[20]

In the Doctrine and Covenants section 138 is recorded perhaps the single greatest doctrine on the subject of the work of the spirit world. It is a vision given to Church President Joseph F. Smith on 3 October 1918. From it, members understand that the faithful, righteous disciples of Christ, who have embraced the fullness of his gospel, teach those spirits who did not have the opportunity to learn of it in life. This is a foundational doctrine that gives life and understanding to most of all other Latter-day Saint beliefs regarding life after death.

In addition to this doctrine, which has come to be known as the "work of salvation for the dead," perhaps the most inspiring and comforting doctrine taught concerning the spirit world (and ultimately the resurrection of the dead) has to do with the joyful reunion that one who dies has with family and friends on the other side of the veil of death. "I have a father, brothers, children, and friends who have gone to a world of spirits," Joseph Smith declared. "They are only absent for a moment; they are in the spirit, and we shall soon meet again. . . . When we depart [from this life], we shall hail our mothers, fathers, friends, and all whom we love who have fallen asleep in Jesus. . . . It will be an eternity of felicity."[21] Brigham Young likewise testified of a glorious reunion with loved ones. "We have more friends behind the vail [of death] than on this side, and they will hail us more joyfully than you were ever welcomed by your parents and friends in this world; and you will rejoice more when you meet them than you ever rejoiced to see a friend in this life."[22]

As cited earlier, one of the core elements of near-death experiences is the encountering of loved ones. It is one of the most commonly cited experiences of those who have in some manner glimpsed beyond the veil of death. Latter-day Saints are drawn to such accounts because they seem to confirm their deep-seated belief in eternal families and "that [the] same sociality," as Joseph Smith characterized it, "which exists among us here will exist among us there, only it will be coupled with eternal glory" (Doctrine and Covenants 130:2).

These are just a few of the Latter-day Saint doctrine and teachings concerning life beyond the grave—like a mere snowflake on the tip of the iceberg. Authors Colleen McDannell and Bernhard Lang commented on the depth and breadth of the Latter-day Saint theology of the afterlife in their book, *Heaven: A History*, published by Yale University Press.

> While most contemporary Christian groups neglect afterlife beliefs, what happens to people after they die is crucial to LDS teachings and rituals. Heavenly theology is the result not of mere speculation, but of revelation given to past and present church leaders. . . .
>
> There has been . . . no alteration of the LDS understanding of the afterlife since its articulation by Joseph Smith. If anything, the Latter-day Saints in the twentieth century have become bolder in their assertion of the importance of their heavenly theology. . . . In the light of what they perceive as a Christian world which has [largely] given up belief in heaven, many Latter-day Saints feel even more responsibility to define the meaning of death and eternal life.[23]

Clearly, it is the similarities with our extensive teachings on the subject that draw Latter-day Saints to the many, many accounts of near-death experiences. Yet doctrine is not the only factor. Latter-day Saints also have a rich historical heritage with the near-death experience phenomenon.

HISTORY

From the earliest days of The Church of Jesus Christ of Latter-day Saints to the present, accounts of near-death or out-of-body experiences have been shared from pulpits—even in the general conferences of the Church, published in official Church publications, discussed in formal Church settings like Sunday School classes as well as in informal settings among friends and neighbors. This historical connection to the phenomenon gives a semblance of credibility and acceptance. No wonder books written by near-death experiencers and those seeking to interpret and give meaning to such experiences, whether authored by members or not, are very popular among Latter-day Saints. Here are just a few examples of this historical pedigree:

- Joseph Smith's mother, Lucy Mack Smith in her *History of Joseph Smith by His Mother* wrote of the powerful impact of the near-death experience that her sister Lovisa Mack Tuttle had in 1784.[24]

- One experience is particularly remarkable. It involves Joseph Smith Jr. himself. Most Latter-day Saints are familiar with an 1832 event in Hiram, Ohio where Joseph was beaten, tarred, and feathered by his enemies. What may not so familiar is the account of Joseph's out-of-body experience at the time. His wife, Emma Hale Smith, remembered:

   The converts to Mr. Smith's preaching were constantly arriving from all parts of the country, [which added] greatly to the disturbance of antagonists to the Mormon religion, and in March, 1832, the most violent persecution followed. Mr. Smith was dragged from his bed, beaten into insensibility, tarred and feathered and left for dead. A strange part of this experience was, that his spirit seemed to leave his body, and that during the period of insensibility he consciously stood over his own body, feeling no pain, but seeing and hearing all that transpired.[25]

- In 1838, Phoebe Woodruff, the wife of Latter-day Saint apostle Wilford Woodruff, became seriously ill and apparently died. Wilford recounted: "The sisters gathered around her body, weeping, while I stood looking at her in sorrow. The spirit and power of God began to rest upon me until, for the first time during her sickness faith filled my soul, although she lay before me as one dead." Woodruff then recounts how he anointed her with oil in the name of the Lord and "rebuked the power of death" and commanded her to be made alive. "Her spirit returned to her body, and from that hour she was made whole." Later Phoebe related to her husband and those present that as she was being anointed with oil, "her spirit left her body, and she saw it lying upon the bed, and the sisters weeping. She looked at them and at [Wilford], and upon her babe, and while gazing upon this scene, two personages came into the room. . . . One of these messengers informed her that she could have her choice: she might go to rest in the spirit world, or, on one condition she could have the privilege of returning to her tabernacle and continuing her labors upon the earth. The condition was, if she felt that she could stand by her husband, and with him pass through all the cares, trials, tribulation, and afflictions of life which he would be called to pass through for the gospel's sake unto the end. When she looked upon the situation of her husband and child, she said: 'Yes, I will do it!' At that moment her spirit [again] entered her tabernacle."[26]

- As the pioneers were crossing the plains, Brigham Young himself experienced two (and possibly more) near-death experiences on 17 February 1847. A seriously ill Brigham Young told his associate and fellow apostle, Willard Richards, "I actually went into Eternity last Wednesday week and came back again."[27] These experiences undoubtedly influenced Young's sermons regarding the conditions of the spirit world, the capacities of departed spirits. He spoke often on the subject. "I can say with regard to parting with our friends, and going ourselves," Young declared in 1871. "I have been near enough to understand eternity so that I have had to exercise a great deal more faith to desire to live that I ever exercised in my whole life to live. The brightness and glory of the next apartment is inexpressible."[28]

- Jedediah M. Grant, second counselor to Brigham Young in the First Presidency of the Church (and father of later Church president, Heber J. Grant), had an extensive near-death experience shortly before his death in 1856. He detailed his experience to President Heber C. Kimball, first counselor in the First Presidency, who publicly recounted it at Grant's funeral:

> He said to me, brother Heber, I have been into the spirit world two nights in succession, and, of all the dreads that ever came across me, the worst was to have to again return to my body, though I had to do it. . . .
>
> [Grant] also spoke of the buildings he saw there, remarking that the Lord gave Solomon wisdom and poured gold and silver into his hands that he might display his skill and ability, and said that the temple erected by Solomon was much

inferior to the most ordinary buildings he saw in the spirit world.

In regards to the gardens, say brother Grant, "I have seen good gardens on this earth, but I never saw any to compare with those that were there. I saw flowers of numerous kinds, and some with fifty to a hundred different colored flowers growing upon one stalk." . . .

After speaking of the gardens and beauty of every thing there, brother Grant said that he felt extremely sorrowful at having to leave so beautiful a place and come back to earth, for he looked upon his body with loathing, but was obliged to enter it again.[29]

- In the late nineteenth century and early twentieth century, numerous near-death experience accounts of prominent Church leaders or their family members such as Lorenzo Dow Young (brother of Brigham Young), George Albert Smith, Jacob Hamblin, George Brimhall, and other Church members were published in the official publications of the Church such as the *Juvenile Instructor*, *Relief Society Magazine, Elders' Journal*, and *Improvement Era*. Additionally, hundreds of spirit world encounters, near-death experiences, or visions can be found in the Church's historical archives.

- A 1920 account of a vision of or encounter with the spirit world by Heber Q. Hale, stake president in Boise, Idaho, is one of the most often quoted accounts. It has been published in a variety of sources. His descriptions of the spirit world correspond remarkably with other accounts, regardless of the denomination.

Although there is long and rich history of Latter-day Saint near-death experiences, it has not always been without controversy. In recent generations, there have been some books containing near-death experiences authored by Church members and published by non-Church publishing outlets that have generated official criticism by the Church and much nonofficial expressions of concern or denunciation in many private circles. In response to one such publication, the Church recently issued the following official statement: "The writings and speculations of individual Church members, some of which have gained currency recently, should be considered as personal accounts or positions that do not reflect Church doctrine."[30] That leads to some general cautions regarding how we (particularly Latter-day Saints) should view near-death experience accounts that are becoming ubiquitous in popular culture.

CAUTIONS

In her foreword to Dr. Raymond Moody's *Life After Life* cited earlier, Elizabeth Kubler-Ross warned that clergy may be upset by his near-death experience research. We have certainly seen that reaction in the forty years since—both in Christianity in general and the Latter-day Saints specifically. Prominent Christian clergy and theologians have railed against the NDE phenomenon. Ironically, many of the latest books and movies are coming from evangelical Christians, much to the chagrin of other evangelicals. Latter-day Saints, despite their doctrine and history regarding the spirit world, have also had their share of similar reactions. Concerns seem to fall into two main categories: (1) the tendency to make the sacred common or, even worse, sensational, and (2) the inclination among some Latter-day Saints (and probably other Christians as well) to seek after these kinds of experiences as a substitute or easy and tantalizing alternative to seeking truth from the word of God, creating, in essence, a kind of "pop" gospel.

While most of these accounts and publications may be intended to inspire and edify, and they often fill that intent, the way some are marketed or publicized seems exploitative, intentionally or unintentionally, and the stories become sensationalized. To the extent that such accounts become popular, one hopes that it is because they are true and good and stimulate believers to more fully study their faith tradition's doctrine and scriptural teachings, and not because they offer an easier or more exciting and engaging version of the gospel than the simple, basic doctrinal teachings about the afterlife.

While NDEs and similar accounts may be interesting and even inspiring to a certain extent, they must never become a substitute for the imperative study and application of the scriptures and prophetic counsel, which are essential to obtaining and maintaining saving faith. Accounts of spiritual encounters with the afterlife cannot change lives and build strength to serve God and resist temptation with the same power and certainty as the word of God.

Furthermore, some of these NDE stories and accounts may set forth mistaken or false doctrines that can lead one astray or mislead others about truth. That is why faithful Latter-day Saints view NDEs only as a side dish, never the main course. They are never an adequate source of doctrine or replacement for faith. Relying only on such fare for one's spiritual nourishment will inevitably cause spiritual starvation. Some things are interesting. Others are imperative.

CONVICTION

Shifting gears from a more academic perspective to a more personal one, let me conclude with my statement of conviction. I have extensively studied near-death experiences in the context of their parallels to Latter-day Saint doctrine for three decades. While my beliefs may be affirmed by such study, my faith does not come from it. My conviction of life after death comes to me from God. Death still hurts. Separation from loved ones is still painful. But I am comforted by my hope for a joyful reunion someday and a glorious resurrection. I add my conviction to these poetic words penned by the late Church President Gordon B. Hinckley:

> What is this thing that men call death,
> This quiet passing in the night?
> 'Tis not the end, but genesis
> Of better worlds and greater light.
> O God, touch Thou my aching heart,
> And calm my troubled, haunting fears.
> Let hope and faith, transcendent, pure,
> Give strength and peace beyond my tears.
> There is no death, but only change
> With recompense for victory won;
> The gift of Him who loved all men,
> The Son of God, the Holy One.[31]

NOTES

1. Elisabeth Kubler-Ross, foreword to *Life After Life* by Raymond A. Moody Jr. (New York: Bantam Books, 1976).
2. Andrew H. Hedges, Alex D. Smith, and Brent M. Rogers, eds., *Journals, Volume 3: May 1843–June 1844*, vol. 3 of the Journals series of *The Joseph Smith Papers*, ed. Ronald K. Esplin and Matthew J. Grow (Salt Lake City: Church Historian's Press, 2015), 109.
3. Orson Pratt, in *Journal of Discourses*, 26 vols. (London: Latter-day Saints' Book Depot, 1854–86), 3:105.
4. "Conference Minutes," *Times and Seasons*, 15 August 1844, 615.
5. The First Presidency (Joseph F. Smith, John R. Winder, Anthon H. Lund), "The Origin of Man," *Improvement Era*, November 1909, 75–81; reprinted in James R. Clark, comp., *Messages of the First Presidency*, 6 vols. (Salt Lake City: Bookcraft, 1965), 4:203–6.
6. The First Presidency, "Origin of Man," 29.
7. Boyd K. Packer, *Teach Ye Diligently* (Salt Lake City: Deseret Book, 2008), 230–37.

8. Brigham Young, in *Journal of Discourses*, 9:287.

9. Quoted in D. Scott Rogo, *The Return from Silence: A Study of Near-Death Experiences* (Wellingborough, Northhamptonshire, England: Aquarian Press, 1989), 162.

10. Emanuel Swedenborg, *Heaven and Hell*, trans. George F. Dole (New York: Swedenborg Foundation, 1990), 70–71.

11. George G. Ritchie Jr., *Return from Tomorrow* (Waco, TX: Chosen Books, 1978), 37–48.

12. Quoted in Carol Zaleski, *Otherworld Journeys: Accounts of Near-Death Experiences in Medieval and Modern Times* (Oxford: Oxford University Press, 1987), 116.

13. John A. Widtsoe, comp., *Discourses of Brigham Young* (Salt Lake City: Deseret Book, 1966), 379.

14. Brigham Young, in *Journal of Discourses*, 13:231.

15. Elizabeth Kubler-Ross, in Zaleski, *Otherworld Journeys*, 116–17.

16. Kenneth Ring and Sharon Cooper, *Mindsight: Near-Death and Out-of-Body Experiences in the Blind* (Palo Alto, CA: William James Center for Consciousness Studies, 1999).

17. Quoted in Moody, *Life After Life*, 53.

18. Joseph Smith, discourse, Nauvoo, Illinois, 9 October 1843, in *Times and Seasons*, 15 September 1843, 331.

19. Sabbath address, Nauvoo, 12 May 1844, as reported by George Laub, Reminiscences and Journal Jan. 1845–Apr. 1857, Church History Library, Salt Lake City.

20. Joseph Smith, discourse, Nauvoo, Illinois, 7 April 1844, *Times and Seasons*, 15 August 1844, 616.

21. Joseph Smith, History, 1838–1856, vol. E-1, created 20 August 1855–5 April 1856, pp. 1977–78.

22. Brigham Young, in *Journal of Discourses*, 6:349.

23. Colleen McDannell and Bernhard Land, *Heaven: A History* (New Haven: Yale University Press, 1988), 312–13.

24. Lucy Mack Smith, *History of Joseph Smith by His Mother, Lucy Mack Smith* (Salt Lake City: Stevens & Wallis, 1945), 12–15.

25. Emma Hale Smith Bidamon, in *Recollections of the Pioneers of Lee County* (Dixon, IL: Inez A. Kennedy, 1893), 98.

26. Wilford Woodruff, *Leaves from My Journal* (Salt Lake City: Juvenile Instructor Office, 1882), 52–55.

27. Willard Richards journal, 28 February 1847, Church History Library, Salt Lake City.

28. Brigham Young, in *Journal of Discourses*, 14:231.

29. Heber C. Kimball, in *Journal of Discourses*, 4:135–36.

30. "Church Responds to Inquiries about Preparedness," Newsroom, churchofjesuschrist.org, 26 September 2015, https://www.mormonnewsroom.org/article/church-responds-to-inquiries-about-preparedness.

31. Gordon B. Hinckley, "The Empty Tomb Bore Testimony," *Ensign*, May 1988, 65–68.

Chapter 7

CHRIST'S DESCENT INTO HELL

A LATTER-DAY SAINT PERSPECTIVE

Robert L. Millet

Robert L. Millet is a Latter-day Saint scholar and a professor emeritus of ancient scripture, Brigham Young University.

A CHALLENGING ISSUE

Since the time of Jesus and the Apostles, theological disputes have been somewhat commonplace, both within the Christian fold and between committed Christians and unbelievers. One of the most difficult questions to answer is called the problem of evil and suffering. In essence, it is as follows: If our God is all-loving, all-knowing, and all-powerful, why is there so much evil and suffering in the world? If God knows of the pain on this planet (because he is omniscient), if he has the power to change things (because he is omnipotent), then how can he be all-loving if he does not in fact bring such pain and anguish to an end?

For now, I would like to turn our attention to a variation of this difficult issue, a challenge that has been called the "soteriological problem of evil." Soteriology is the study of salvation—what it is and how it comes to the children of God. The soteriological problem of evil has been described by one theologian through a question:

> What is the fate of those who die never hearing of the gospel of Christ? Are all the "heathen" lost? Is there an opportunity for those who have never heard of Jesus to be saved?
>
> These questions raise one of the most perplexing, provocative and perennial issues facing Christians. It has been considered by philosophers and farmers, Christians and non-Christians. . . . Far and away, this is the most-asked apologetic question on U.S. College campuses. . . .
>
> Although there is no way of knowing exactly how many people died without ever hearing about Israel or the church, it seems safe to conclude that the vast majority of human beings who have ever lived fall into this category.
>
> In terms of sheer numbers, then, an inquiry into the salvation of the unevangelized is of immense interest. What may be said about the destiny of countless billions who have lived and died apart from any understanding of the divine grace manifested in Jesus?[1]

Christian apologist C. S. Lewis found himself puzzled by this dilemma. On one occasion he remarked: "Here is [a matter] that used to puzzle me. Is it not frightfully unfair that this new life [in Christ] should be confined to people who have heard of Christ and been able to believe in Him? But the truth is God has not told us what His arrangements about the other people are. We do know that no man can be saved except through Christ; we do not know that only those who know Him can be saved through Him."[2]

With the soteriological problem of evil before us, let me address this matter from a Latter-day Saint perspective. My remarks will focus primarily on the continuation of Christ's ministry following his death on the cross and what has come to be known in Christian history as his "descent into hell" between the time of his death and his resurrection from the dead.

EARLY CHRISTIAN TEACHINGS

Early in Jesus's ministry, a group of Pharisees, no doubt well aware of the miracles he had performed, made a request. "Master," they began, "we would see a sign from thee." Now note his prompt response: "An evil and adulterous generation seeketh after a sign." Most of us are happy to stop there in the narrative and smile at the Master's boldness. But, of course, the account does not end there, for Jesus continued: "And there shall be no sign given to it, but the sign of the prophet Jonas: for as Jonas was three days and three nights in the whale's belly; *so shall the Son of man be three days and three nights in the heart of the earth*" (Matthew 12:38–40; emphasis added). The Apostle Paul emphasized that "Christ both died, and rose, and revived, that he might be Lord both of the dead and living" (Romans 14:9). More particularly, Paul wrote to the Ephesians that before Christ "ascended up on high" to "[lead] captivity captive," he "descended first into the lower parts of the earth" (Ephesians 4:8–9). That is the King James Version. The New Jerusalem Bible renders it as follows: "When it says 'he went up', it must mean that he had gone down to the deepest levels of the earth" (Ephesians 4:9).

Several of the early church fathers taught that "no one, on becoming absent from the body, is at once a dweller in the presence of the Lord."[3] Early in the second century following Christ, Justin Martyr (ca. AD 160) noted, "The souls of the godly remain in a better place, while those of the unjust and wicked are in a worse place, waiting for the time of judgment."[4] Clement of Alexandria (ca. AD 195) attested that Jesus "descended to Hades . . . to preach the Gospel" and that "all who believe will be saved on making their profession there." This is because, Clement continued, "God's punishments are saving and disciplinary, leading to conversion. He desires the repentance, rather than the death, of a sinner. This is especially so since *souls, although darkened by passions, when released from their bodies, are able to perceive more clearly*. For they are no longer obstructed by the paltry flesh."[5] Further, "it is not here alone that the active power of God is present. Rather, it is everywhere and is always at work. . . . For it is not right that those persons [who died before Christ] should be condemned without trial, and that those alone who lived after His coming should have the advantage of the divine righteousness."[6] In summary, as Irenaus (ca. AD 180) noted, "the souls of His [Christ's] disciples also (upon whose account the Lord underwent these things) will go away into the invisible place allotted to them by God. And they will remain there until the resurrection, awaiting that event."[7]

We read a description in the entry "Descent into Hell" from a respected Bible dictionary: "a widely held belief in the early Church, and later an article of the Apostles' Creed, that between his crucifixion and resurrection Jesus descended into the underworld (Hades) either to proclaim victory, to release OT saints, or to proclaim the gospel. Such beliefs and their later creedal development emphasized the universality of salvation offered in Jesus Christ."[8] The *Catechism of the Catholic Church* states that "the crucified one sojourned in the realm of the dead prior to his resurrection. This was the first meaning given in the apostolic preaching to Christ's descent into hell: that Jesus, like all men, experienced death and in his soul joined the others in the realm of the dead. But he descended there as Savior, proclaiming the good news to the spirits imprisoned there."[9]

THE LATTER-DAY SAINT PERSPECTIVE UNFOLDS

While the Joseph Smith Sr. family read the Bible together and had frequent discussions on religious matters, it is probably the case that young Joseph Smith encountered what we know as the gospel of Jesus Christ largely in his translation of the Book of Mormon. What did he learn from the Book of Mormon about salvation for all people? He learned that baptism is an essential ordinance (sacrament), one that must be properly performed to admit a person into the kingdom of God (2 Nephi 31; Mosiah 18). He learned that "this life is the time for men to prepare to meet God; yea, behold the day of this life is the day for men to perform their labors," and that "after this day of life, which is given us to prepare for eternity, behold, if we do not improve our time while in this life, then cometh the night of darkness wherein there can be no labor performed" (Alma 34:32–33). Like the book of Deuteronomy, the Book of Mormon essentially sets forth the doctrine of the two ways: things are either black or white, good or evil, and our choices lead either to blessing or to cursing.

A significant moment in Latter-day Saint history and theology unfolded in the fall of 1833 in the life of a woman by the name of Lydia Goldthwaite. Lydia grew up in Massachusetts and New York and at the age of sixteen married Calvin Bailey. Calvin had a serious drinking problem and eventually left Lydia and their child. At the time, Lydia was also expecting another baby. The baby died at birth, and within months her first child died also. When she was twenty years old, Lydia moved to Canada to stay with the Freeman Nickerson family. There she was introduced to The Church of Jesus Christ of Latter-day Saints and first became acquainted with Joseph Smith. On 24 October 1833 the family sat around the table and listened to Joseph. Those who recorded this event reported that the Spirit of God was poured out upon the group in a remarkable manner, and Lydia even spoke in tongues. The next day, as Joseph's company prepared to return to Kirtland, Ohio, the Prophet

> paced back and forth in the sitting room in deep study. Finally he spoke up and said: "I have been pondering on Sister Lydia's lonely condition, and wondering why it is that she has passed through so much sorrow and affliction and is thus separated from all her relatives. I now understand it. The Lord has suffered it even as he allowed Joseph of old to be afflicted, who was sold by his brethren as a slave into a far country, and through that became a savior to his father's house and country. . . . Even so shall it be with her; the hand of the Lord will overrule it for good to her and her father's family."
>
> Turning to the young girl he continued: "Sister Lydia, great are your blessings. The Lord, your Savior, loves you, and will overrule all your past sorrows and afflictions for good unto you. Let your heart be comforted. . . . You shall yet be a savior to your father's house. Therefore be comforted, and let your heart rejoice, for the

Lord has a great work for you to do. Be faithful and endure unto the end and all will be well."[10]

Almost three years later, on 21 January 1836, the following event occurred:

> At early candlelight I [Joseph Smith] met with the [First] presidency, at the west school room, in the [Kirtland, Ohio] Temple, to attend to the ordinance of anointing our heads with holy oil: Also the [High] councils of Kirtland and Zion met in the two adjoining rooms, who waited in prayer while we attended to the ordinance. I took the oil in my left hand, Father Smith [Joseph Smith Sr.] being seated before me, and the remainder of the Presidency encircled him round about. We then stretched our right hands towards heaven, and blessed the oil, and consecrated it in the name of Jesus Christ. We then laid our hands on our aged Father Smith, and invoked the blessings of heaven. . . . The [First] presidency then . . . received their anointing and blessing under the hand, of father Smith. . . . All of the [First] Presidency laid th[e]ir hands upon me, and pronounced upon my head many prophecies, and blessings, many of which I shall not notice at this time. But as Paul said, so say I, let us come to visions and revelations.[11]

Brother Joseph states: "The heavens were opened upon us, and I beheld the celestial kingdom of God [the highest heaven], and the glory thereof, whether in the body or out I cannot tell. I saw the transcendent beauty of the gate through which the heirs of that kingdom will enter, which was like unto circling flames of fire; also the blazing throne of God, whereon was seated the Father and the Son. I saw the beautiful streets of that kingdom, which had the appearance of being paved with gold" (Doctrine and Covenants 137:1–4). Joseph Smith's description of the celestial kingdom was not unlike John the Revelator's vision of the holy city, the earth in its sanctified state: "The foundations of the wall of the city," wrote John, "were garnished with all manner of precious stones." Further, "the street of the city was pure gold, as it were transparent glass" (Revelation 21:19, 21).

Joseph's account of the vision continues: "I saw Father Adam and Abraham; and my father and my mother; my brother Alvin, that has long since slept; and marveled how it was that he [Alvin] had obtained an inheritance in that kingdom, seeing that he had departed this life before the Lord had set his hand to gather Israel the second time, and had not been baptized for the remission of sins" (Doctrine and Covenants 137:5–6).

Clearly, this was a glimpse into a future heaven, for he saw his parents in the kingdom of the just, when in fact both were still living in 1836. Joseph Sr. would not die until 1840, and Mother Smith would live for another twenty years. Father Smith was, as we mentioned earlier, in the same room with his son at the time the vision was received.

Joseph's brother Alvin was the firstborn of Joseph Sr. and Lucy Mack Smith. He was born on 11 February 1798 in Tunbridge, Vermont. Lucy Mack Smith wrote that on the morning of 15 November 1823, "Alvin was taken very sick with the bilious colic," which was probably appendicitis. A physician hurried to the Smith home and administered calomel, an experimental drug. The dose of calomel "lodged in his stomach," and on the third day of sickness Alvin became aware that he was going to die. He asked that each of the Smith children come to his bedside for his parting counsel and final expression of love. According to Mother Smith's record, "When he came to Joseph, he said, 'I am now going to die, the distress which I suffer, and the feelings that I have, tell me my time is very short. I want you to be . . . faithful in receiving instruction, and in keeping every commandment that is given you.'"[12]

Alvin died on 19 November 1823. Mother Smith wrote of the pall of grief surrounding his passing: "Alvin was a youth of singular goodness of disposition—kind and amiable, so that lamentation and mourning filled the whole neighborhood in which he resided."[13] Joseph commented later: "I remember well the pangs of sorrow that swelled my youthful bosom and almost burst my tender heart when he died. He was the oldest and noblest of my father's family. . . . He lived without spot from the time he was a child. . . . He was one of the soberest of men, and when he died the angel of the Lord visited him in his last moments."[14]

Because Alvin had died seven years before the organization of The Church of Jesus Christ of Latter-day Saints and had not been baptized, Joseph wondered during his vision how it was possible for his brother to have attained the highest heaven. Alvin's family had been shocked and saddened at his funeral by the remarks of a local minister. William Smith, Alvin's younger brother, recalled: "Hyrum, Samuel, Katherine, and mother were members of the Presbyterian Church. My father would not join. He did not like it because Rev. Stockton had preached at my brother's funeral sermon and intimated very strongly that he had gone to hell, for Alvin was not a church member, but he was a good boy and my father did not like it."[15] What consolation must have filled the souls of both Joseph Smith Jr. and Sr. when the voice of God declared, "All who have died without a knowledge of this gospel, who would have received it if they had been permitted to tarry, shall be heirs of the celestial kingdom of God; also all that shall die henceforth without a knowledge of it, who would have received it with all their hearts, shall be heirs of that kingdom; for I, the Lord, will judge all men according to their works, according to the desire of their hearts" (Doctrine and Covenants 137:7–9).

The principle that God does not hold anyone accountable for a gospel law of which he or she was ignorant had actually been taught in the Book of Mormon (2 Nephi 9:25–26; Mosiah 3:11; 15:24). Joseph learned in this vision that every person will have an opportunity—here or hereafter—to accept and apply the principles of the gospel of Jesus Christ. Only God is capable of perfect judgment, and thus only he can discern completely the hearts and minds of mortal men and women. He alone knows when a person has received sufficient knowledge or impressions of the Spirit to constitute a valid opportunity to receive the message of salvation. This vision reaffirmed that the Lord will judge men not only by their actions but also by their attitudes—the desires of their heart (see also Alma 41:3).

Another of the fascinating doctrines enunciated in what Latter-day Saints call the vision of the celestial kingdom deals with the status of children who die. "And I also beheld," Joseph stated, "that all children who die before they arrive at the years of accountability are saved in the celestial kingdom of heaven" (Doctrine and Covenants 137:10). This part of the vision confirmed what Book of Mormon prophets had taught. One religious leader, King Benjamin, declared that "the infant perisheth not that dieth in his infancy" (Mosiah 3:18). Another prophet, Abinadi, said simply: "Little children also have eternal life" (Mosiah 15:25). A revelation given to Joseph Smith in September 1830 had specified that "little children are redeemed from the foundation of the world through mine Only Begotten" (Doctrine and Covenants 29:46). Joseph later taught that "the Lord takes many away, even in infancy, that they may escape the envy of man, and the sorrows and evils of this present world; they were too pure, too lovely, to live on earth; therefore, if rightly considered, instead of mourning we have reason to rejoice as they are delivered from evil, and we shall soon have them again."[16] A twentieth-century Latter-day Saint leader explained that by virtue of the Lord's infinite understanding of the human family, "we must assume that the Lord knows and arranges beforehand who shall be taken in infancy and who shall remain on earth to undergo whatever tests are needed in their cases."[17]

THE REDEMPTION OF THE DEAD

On the afternoon of Tuesday, 8 May 1838, the Prophet Joseph answered a series of questions about the faith and practices of the Latter-day Saints. One of the questions was: "If the Mormon doctrine is true what has become of all those who died since the days of the apostles[?]" Joseph's response: "All those who have not had an opportunity of hearing the gospel, and being administered to by an inspired man in the flesh, must have it hereafter, before they can be finally judged."[18] We cannot help but conclude that Joseph must have spoken of this doctrinal matter since the time of his vision of Alvin more than two years earlier, but there is no record of such a conversation.

The first public discourse on the subject by the Prophet was delivered on 15 August 1840 at the funeral of a man named Seymour Brunson.[19] Simon Baker described the occasion: "I was present at a discourse that the prophet Joseph delivered on baptism for the dead 15 August 1840. He read the greater part of the 15th chapter of Corinthians and remarked that the Gospel of Jesus Christ brought glad tidings of great joy, and then remarked that he saw a widow in that congregation that had a son who died without being baptized, and this widow [had read] the sayings of Jesus 'except a man be born of water and of the spirit he cannot enter the kingdom of heaven. . . .' He then said that this widow should have glad tidings in that thing. He also said the apostle [Paul] was talking to a people who understood baptism for the dead, for it was practiced among them [see 1 Corinthians 15:29]. He went on to say that people could now act for their friends who had departed this life, and that the plan of salvation was calculated to save all who were willing to obey the requirements of the law of God. He went on and made a very beautiful discourse."[20]

After the meeting, a widow, Jane Nyman, was baptized vicariously for her son in the Mississippi River.[21] Just one month later, on 14 September 1840, on his death bed, Joseph Smith Sr. made a final request of his family—that someone be baptized in behalf of his eldest son, Alvin. His second son, Hyrum, complied with that wish and was baptized vicariously in 1840 in the Mississippi River and again in 1841 in a baptismal font in the Nauvoo Temple.[22]

In an epistle dated 19 October 1840, Joseph Smith stated: "I presume the doctrine of 'baptism for the dead' has ere this reached your ears, and may have raised some inquiries in your minds respecting the same. I cannot in this letter give you all the information you may desire on the subject; but aside from knowledge independent of the Bible, I would say that it was certainly practised by the Ancient Churches." The Prophet then quoted from 1 Corinthians 15:29 and continued: "I first mentioned the doctrine in public, when preaching the funeral sermon of Brother Seymour Brunson, and have since then given general instructions in the Church on the subject. The Saints have the privilege of being baptized for those of their relatives who are dead, who they believe would have embraced the gospel, if they had been privileged with hearing it, and who have received the gospel in the Spirit, through the instrumentality of those who have been commissioned to preach to them while in prison."[23]

On 20 March 1842 the Prophet stated that if we have the authority to perform valid baptisms for the living, it is our responsibility to make those same blessings available to those who have passed through death.[24] One month later, in an editorial in the Nauvoo newspaper, *Times and Seasons*, Joseph called upon the Saints to expand their vision concerning the purposes of God. "While one portion of the human race are judging and condemning the other without mercy," he said, "the great parent of the universe looks upon the whole of the human family with a fatherly care, and paternal regard; he views them as his offspring, and without any of those contracted feelings that influence the children of men." He observed that "it is an opinion which is generally received, that the destiny of man is irretrievably fixed at his death; and that he is made either eternally happy, or eternally miserable; that if a man dies without a knowledge of God, he must be eternally damned. . . . Our Saviour says that all manner of sin, and blasphemy shall be forgiven men wherewith they shall blaspheme; but the blasphemy against the Holy Ghost shall not be forgiven, neither in *this world*, nor in the *world to come*, evidently showing that *there are sins which may be forgiven in the world to come*." To this doctrinal statement, Joseph added: "The great Jehovah contemplated the whole of the events connected with the earth, [and] the past, present and the future, were, and are with him one eternal now." Moreover, Brother Joseph stated, "Chrysostum [AD 349–407] says that the Marcionites practiced baptism for the dead. . . . The church of course at that time was degenerate, and the particular form might be incorrect, but the thing is sufficiently plain in the scriptures." He again quoted

1 Corinthians 15:29 and concluded by referring to the restoration of this dimension of the "ancient order of things" as the fulfillment of the words of Obadiah concerning persons becoming "saviors . . . on Mount Zion" (Obadiah 1:21). "A view of these things reconciles the scriptures of truth, justifies the ways of God to man; places the human family upon an equal footing, and harmonizes with every principle of righteousness, justice, and truth."[25]

CHRIST'S POSTMORTAL MINISTRY

On 2 May 1844, Joseph Smith summarized the principle: *"Every man that has been baptized and belongs to the kingdom has a right to be baptized for those who have gone before; and as soon as the law of the Gospel is obeyed here by their friends who act as proxy for them, the Lord has administrators there to set them free."*[26] Consequently, Latter-day Saints believe and teach that the disembodied Christ visited the postmortal spirit world and taught his gospel and that after his departure from the spirit world and his resurrection others were commissioned and empowered to continue that work. Latter-day Saints believe this is attested in the following words of Peter's first epistle: "For Christ also hath once suffered for sins, the just [the Lord] for the unjust [you and me], that he might bring us to God, being put to death in the flesh, but quickened by the Spirit: by which also he went and preached unto the spirits in prison; which sometime were disobedient, when once the longsuffering of God waited in the days of Noah, while the ark was a preparing, wherein few, that is, eight souls were saved by water" (1 Peter 3:18–20). In the very next chapter of the epistle, Peter teaches that all people must one day give an accounting of their lives before the Lord, who will "judge the quick and the dead." Then comes this verse: "For for this cause was the gospel preached also to them that are dead, that they might be judged according to men in the flesh, but live according to God in the spirit" (1 Peter 4:5–6). From our point of view, because God is both merciful and just, every man and woman who live on planet earth will have the opportunity, either in this world or in the world to come, to hear and accept the message that salvation comes only by and through the Atonement of the Lord Jesus Christ.[27]

On 3 October 1918, Joseph F. Smith, nephew of Joseph Smith and himself sixth President of the Church, sat reflecting on these very verses from Peter's first epistle. In speaking of what then occurred, Joseph F. explained: "As I pondered over these things which are written, the eyes of my understanding were opened, and the Spirit of the Lord rested upon me, and I saw the hosts of the dead, both small and great." More specifically, he was permitted to witness scenes of what life was like in the postmortal spirit world among the noble and righteous, "an innumerable company of the spirits of the just," at the time Jesus died and entered the spirit world. "I beheld that they were filled with joy and gladness, and were rejoicing together because the day of their deliverance was at hand. They were assembled awaiting the advent of the Son of God into the spirit world, to declare their redemption from the bands of death. Their sleeping dust was to be restored unto its perfect frame, bone to his bone, and the sinews and the flesh upon them, the spirit and the body to be united never again to be divided, that they might receive a fullness of joy. While this vast multitude waited and conversed, rejoicing in the hour of their deliverance from the chains of death, the Son of God appeared, declaring liberty to the captives who had been faithful; and there he preached to them the everlasting gospel, the doctrine of the resurrection and the redemption of mankind from the fall, and from individual sins on conditions of repentance" (Doctrine and Covenants 138:11–12, 15–19).

This was in harmony with, and a confirmation of, what his uncle Joseph Smith had taught some eighty years earlier. Having had that particular insight affirmed, Joseph F. wondered how it was possible, then, for the disembodied Savior to minister to so many in so short a time (between his death and his resurrection). "And as I wondered," he continued, "my eyes were opened, and my understanding quickened, and I perceived that the Lord went not in person among the wicked and the disobedient who had rejected the truth, to teach them; but behold, *from among the righteous, he organized his forces and appointed messengers, clothed with power and authority, and commissioned them to go forth and carry the light of the gospel to them that were in darkness, even to all the spirits of men*; and thus was the gospel preached to the dead" (Doctrine and Covenants 138:29–30; emphasis added). This significant detail is nowhere found in the sermons or writings of his uncle. Joseph F. also states the matter here: *"Unto the wicked he did not go, and among the ungodly and the unrepentant who had defiled themselves while in the flesh, his voice was not raised. . . .* Where these were, darkness reigned, but among the righteous there was peace" (Doctrine and Covenants 138:20, 22; emphasis added). It is interesting to consider the following Roman Catholic teaching: "Jesus did not descend into hell to deliver the damned, nor to destroy the hell of damnation, but to free the just who had gone before him."[28]

"THIS DAY . . . IN PARADISE"

On Golgotha, Jesus hung on the cross between two thieves. One of them "railed on him, saying, If thou be Christ, save thyself and us. But the other answering rebuked him, saying, Dost not thou fear God, seeing thou art in the same condemnation? And we indeed justly; for we receive the due reward of our deeds: but this man hath done nothing amiss. And he said unto Jesus, Lord, remember me when thou comest into thy kingdom. And Jesus said unto him, Verily I say unto thee, To day shalt thou be with me in paradise" (Luke 23:39–43).

As we might expect, this passage has given rise to a whole host of interpretations, perhaps the most prevalent being a belief in a type of deathbed confession and repentance. To be sure, it is good to repent no matter *when* we do it. That is, it is better to repent than to remain in our sins. Joseph Smith himself taught, "There is never a time when the spirit is too old to approach God. All are within the reach of pardoning mercy, who have not committed the unpardonable sin."[29] On another occasion, however, he taught, "We should take warning and not wait for the death-bed to repent. . . . Let this, then, prove as a warning to all not to procrastinate repentance, or wait till a death-bed, for it is the will of God that man should repent and serve Him in health, and in the strength and power of his mind, in order to secure His blessing, and not wait until he is called to die."[30]

Respected New Testament scholar N. T. Wright pointed out that "the early Christian future hope centered firmly on resurrection. The first Christians did not simply believe in life after death; they virtually never spoke simply of going to heaven when they died. . . . When they did speak of heaven as a postmortem destination, they seemed to regard this heavenly life as a temporary stage on the way to the resurrection of the body. When Jesus tells the brigand [thief on the cross] that he will join him in paradise that very day, paradise clearly cannot be their ultimate destination, as Luke's next chapter [where the resurrected Lord appears to many] makes clear."[31] In short, for Wright, the mention of resurrection "wasn't a way of talking about life after death. It was a way of talking about a new bodily life *after* whatever state of existence one might enter immediately upon death." That is, resurrection and glory are "life *after* life after death."[32]

Joseph Smith stated: "I will say something about the spirits in prison. There has been much said by modern divines about the words of Jesus (when on the cross) to the thief, saying, 'This day shalt thou be with me in paradise.' King James' translators make it out to say paradise. But what is paradise? It is a modern [Persian] word: it does not answer at all to the original word that Jesus made use of [presumably the word *hades*]. Find the original of the word paradise. You might as easily find a needle in a haymow. . . . There is nothing in the original word in Greek from which this was taken that signifies paradise; but it was—This day thou shalt be with me *in the world of spirits*.'"[33]

Josiah Quincy, a man who later became the mayor of Boston, visited the Prophet Joseph in Nauvoo and wrote later of an occasion wherein Joseph spoke on the necessity of baptism for salvation. A minister in the audience contended as follows with Joseph:

Minister. Stop! What do you say to the case of the penitent thief?
Prophet. What do you mean by that? *Minister.* You know our
Saviour said to the thief, "This day shalt thou be with me in Paradise," which shows he could not have been baptized before his
admission. *Prophet.* How do you know he wasn't baptized before he
became a thief? At this retort the sort of laugh that is provoked by
an unexpected hit ran through the audience; but this demonstration of sympathy was rebuked by a severe look from Smith, who
went on to say: "But that is not the true answer. In the original
Greek, as this gentleman [turning to me] will inform you, the word
that has been translated paradise means simply a place of departed
spirits. To that place the penitent thief was conveyed."[34]

Three questions are frequently asked about the Latter-day Saint
doctrine of the hereafter. First, are the Latter-day Saints universalists?
No, not if that means that all men and women will eventually be saved in
the highest heaven, for that would be at variance with our doctrine. No,
in that we believe, with our Christian brothers and sisters, that salvation
is in Christ and in him alone and that no man or woman will inherit the
highest glory hereafter who does not accept Jesus as the Christ, the Son
of God, the Savior and Redeemer, and with that acceptance receive his
gospel, including the covenants and ordinances (sacraments) associated
with entering into the Lord's Church and kingdom. We do, however,
believe that all will be saved in a kingdom of glory hereafter, except for
those known as the sons of perdition.[35]

Second, do the Latter-day Saints believe in "hell"? Yes, but for us
hell is a condition, a state of mind, as well as a place within the postmortal spirit world. A revelation given to Joseph Smith describes the
kind of people who will enter hell at death: "These are they who received
not the gospel of Christ, neither the testimony of Jesus, . . . neither the
prophets, neither the everlasting covenant. . . . These are they who are
liars, and sorcerers, and adulterers, and whoremongers," and murderers.
"These are they who suffer the wrath of God on earth," meaning who will
be destroyed by the brightness and glory of Christ at his Second Coming.

"These are they who suffer the vengeance of eternal fire. These are they who are cast down to hell and suffer the wrath of Almighty God, until the fulness of times, when Christ shall have subdued all enemies under his feet, and shall have perfected his work" (Doctrine and Covenants 76:82, 101, 103–6; see also Revelation 21:8; 22:15 relative to murderers). They "deny not the Holy Spirit" (Doctrine and Covenants 76:83). That is, their wickedness is not such as to lead to complete perdition; at the time of their mortal death, they enter into that realm of the postmortal sphere we know as hell and are confronted with their sinfulness. These do not come out of hell until they come forth in the "last resurrection," at the end of the Millennium (Doctrine and Covenants 76:85). Thus, the only ones to experience eternal hell are the sons of perdition.

And what of the lake of fire and brimstone into which the wicked are cast? Joseph Smith taught: "The great misery of departed spirits in the world of spirits, where they go after death, is to know that they come short of the glory that others enjoy and that they might have enjoyed themselves, and they are their own accusers." Further: "A man is his own tormentor and his own condemner. Hence the saying, They shall go into the lake that burns with fire and brimstone [see Revelation 21:8]. The torment of disappointment in the mind of man is as exquisite as a lake burning with fire and brimstone. I say, so is the torment of man."[36]

Third, where do the Latter-day Saints get their notion of more heavens than one? While meeting with his chosen disciples at the Last Supper, the Master said: "Let not your heart be troubled: ye believe in God, believe also in me. In my Father's house are many mansions: if it were not so, I would have told you. I go to prepare a place for you" (John 14:1–2). This is a most intriguing statement. From a Latter-day Saint perspective, the Savior seems to have been saying, in essence, that it should be obvious to anyone that life hereafter consists of more than merely a heaven and a hell; if it were not so, he would have told us otherwise. Reason suggests that not all people are equally good and thus not all good people deserve the same reward hereafter. Likewise, not all bad people are equally bad and surely some are so bad they deserve to sink to the lowest pit in hell.

Just how unusual is this notion of degrees of glory? St. Augustine wrote: "Who can conceive, not to say describe, what degrees of honor and glory shall be awarded to the various degrees of merit? Yet it cannot be doubted that there shall be degrees. And in that blessed city there shall be this great blessing, that no inferior shall envy any superior, as now the archangels are not envied by the angels, because no one will wish to be what he has not received. . . . And thus, along with this gift, greater or less, each shall receive this further gift of contentment to desire no more than he has.[37]

During the First Great Awakening, American theologian Jonathan Edwards, stated: "There are many mansions in God's house because heaven is intended for various degrees of honor and blessedness. Some are designed to sit in higher places there than others; some are designed to be advanced to higher degrees of honor and glory than others are."[38] Similarly, John Wesley, essentially the father of Methodism, spoke of some persons enjoying "higher degrees of glory" hereafter. "There is an inconceivable variety in the degrees of reward in the other world. . . . In worldly things men are ambitious to get as high as they can. Christians have a far more noble ambition. The difference between the very highest and the lowest state in the world is nothing to the smallest difference between the degrees of glory."[39]

CONCLUSION

Frederic W. Farrar observed that "St. Peter has one doctrine that is almost peculiar to himself, and which is inestimably precious." This doctrine, Farrar added, is a "much-disregarded, and, indeed, till recent times half-forgotten, article of the Christian creed;—I mean the object of Christ's descent into Hades. In this truth is involved nothing less than the extension of Christ's redeeming work to the dead who died before His coming." Farrar then quoted 1 Peter 3:18–20 and 1 Peter 4:6

and stated: "Few words of Scripture have been so tortured and emptied of their significance as these." He noted that "every effort has been made to explain away the plain meaning of this passage. It is one of the most precious passages of Scripture, and it involves no ambiguity, except such as is created by the scholasticism of a prejudiced theology. It stands almost alone in Scripture. . . . For if language have any meaning, *this language means that Christ, when His Spirit descended into the lower world, proclaimed the message of salvation to the once impenitent dead.*" And then, in broadening our perspective beyond those of the days of Noah, Farrar wrote: "But *it is impossible to suppose that the antediluvian sinners, conspicuous as they were for their wickedness, were the only ones of all the dead who were singled out to receive the message of deliverance.*" Continuing, the revered churchman pointed out: "We thus rescue the work of redemption from the appearance of having failed to achieve its end for the vast majority of those for whom Christ died. By accepting the light thus thrown upon 'the descent into Hell,' we extend to those of the dead who have not finally hardened themselves against it the blessedness of Christ's atoning work." Later Farrar wrote that "we do not press the inference of Hermas and St. Clemens of Alexandria by teaching that this passage implies also *other* missions of Apostles and Saints to the world of spirits."[40] As stated in the *Catechism of the Catholic Church*, "The descent into hell brings the Gospel message of salvation to complete fulfillment. This is the last phase of Jesus' messianic message, a phase which is condensed in time but vast in its real significance."[41]

"We are frequently asked the question," Joseph Smith once said, "what has become of our fathers? Will they all be damned for not obeying the Gospel, when they never heard it? Certainly not. But they will possess the same privilege that we here enjoy, through the medium of the everlasting priesthood, which not only administers on earth, but also in heaven, and the wise dispensations of the great Jehovah."[42]

Latter-day Saints' hope in Christ is in the infinite capacity of an infinite Being to save men and women from ignorance as well as from sin and death. The God of Abraham, Isaac, and Jacob is indeed the God of the living (Matthew 22:32), and his influence and redemptive mercies span the veil of death. The Apostle Paul wrote that "if in this life only we have hope in Christ, we are of all men most miserable" (1 Corinthians 15:19).

So what of those who never have the opportunity in this life to know of Christ and his gospel, who never have the opportunity to be baptized for a remission of sins and for entrance into the kingdom of God? Joseph Smith's answer: "All those who have not had an opportunity of hearing the Gospel, and being administered unto by an inspired man in the flesh, *must have it hereafter, before they can be finally judged.*"[43] In other words, Joseph Smith remarked, "It is no more incredible that God should *save* the dead, than that he should *raise* the dead."[44]

NOTES

1. John Sanders, ed., *What About Those Who Have Never Heard?* (Downers Grove, IL: InterVarsity Press, 1995), 7–9; see also Clark Pinnock and Delwin Brown, *Theological Crossfire* (Grand Rapids, MI: Zondervan, 1990), 227.

2. C. S. Lewis, *Mere Christianity* (New York: Touchstone, 1996), 65.

3. Tertullian, in *The Ante-Nicene Fathers*, ed. Alexander Roberts and James Donaldson, 10 vols. (Peabody, MA: Hendrickson, 1994), 3:576.

4. Roberts and Donaldson, *Ante-Nicene Fathers*, 1:197.

5. Roberts and Donaldson, *Ante-Nicene Fathers*, 2:490–91; emphasis added.

6. Roberts and Donaldson, *Ante-Nicene Fathers*, 2:490–91.

7. Roberts and Donaldson, *Ante-Nicene Fathers*, 1:560.

8. Iain S. Maclain, "Descent into Hell," in *Eerdmans Dictionary of the Bible*, ed. David Noel Freedman (Grand Rapids, MI: Eerdmans, 2000), 338.

9. *Catechism of the Catholic Church* (New York: Doubleday, 1995), part 1, article 5, paragraph 1, 180.

10. "Lydia Knight's History," 21–23, cited in Journal History of The Church of Jesus Christ of Latter-day Saints, 19 October 1833, Church History Library, Salt Lake City.

11. Joseph Smith, History, 1838–1856, vol. B-1, created 1 October 1843–24 February 1845; referring to 2 Corinthians 12:1–5.

12. Preston Nibley, ed., *History of Joseph Smith by His Mother* (Salt Lake City: Bookcraft, n.d.), 87.

13. Nibley, *History of Joseph Smith by His Mother*, 88.

14. *Teachings of Presidents of the Church: Joseph Smith* (Salt Lake City: The Church of Jesus Christ of Latter-day Saints, 2007), 485; cited hereafter as *Joseph Smith*, followed by the page number.

15. William Smith, interview by E. C. Briggs and J. W. Peterson, in *Deseret News*, 20 January 1894; see also Kyle R. Walker, *William Smith: In the Shadow of a Prophet* (Salt Lake City: Greg Kofford Books, 2015), 50.

16. *Joseph Smith*, 176.

17. Bruce R. McConkie, expressing the sentiments of Joseph Fielding Smith, in "The Salvation of Little Children," *Ensign*, April 1977, 6.

18. *Elders' Journal* 1, no. 2 (July 1838): 43.

19. *Joseph Smith*, 472.

20. Andrew F. Ehat and Lyndon W. Cook , eds., *The Words of Joseph Smith: The Contemporary Accounts of the Nauvoo Discourses of the Prophet Joseph* (Provo, UT: Religious Studies Center, Brigham Young University, 1980), 49.

21. See Alex Baugh, "The Practice of Baptism for the Dead Outside of Temples," *Religious Studies Center Newsletter* 13, no. 1 (September 1998): 3–6.

22. "Nauvoo Baptisms for the Dead," Book A, Family History Library, Salt Lake City, 145, 149.

23. Joseph Smith, History, 1838–1856, vol. C-1, created 24 February 1845– 3 July 1845.

24. *Joseph Smith*, 472.

25. Editorial, *Times and Seasons*, 15 April 1842, 760–61.

26. *Joseph Smith*, 474; emphasis added.

27. Obviously, the passages in 1 Peter are not understood in the same way by all Christian groups. A Roman Catholic view is that Christ went to the abode of Saints who had already lived and died and taught them his gospel—that he had conquered sin, death, and hell. Christ then led them out of that place. A Lutheran interpretation is that our Lord descended to Hades to declare his victory over and to pronounce condemnation upon Satan. A fairly traditional Anglican point of view is that following his death on the cross, Jesus went to Hades to that part called paradise and there delivered to the righteous a more complete understanding of the gospel. Some Evangelical interpretations include: (1) a "pre-incarnate prophetic ministry of Jesus"

to those who had died in the days of Noah and the flood, (2) Peter's reference to the people in the days of Noah is figurative or symbolic, pointing to the fact that many in the days of Jesus were as unbelieving and rebellious as those in the days of Noah, (3) the "spirits in prison" are simply those who were in bondage to sin and ignorance during the Savior's mortal ministry. See Millard J. Ericson, *Christian Theology* (Grand Rapids, MI: Baker Book House, 1986); John MacArthur, *The MacArthur Bible Commentary* (Nashville: Thomas Nelson Publishers, 2005), 1915–17.

28. *Catechism of the Catholic Church*, part 1, section 2, article 5, 180.

29. *Joseph Smith*, 76, 471.

30. *Joseph Smith*, 73.

31. N. T. Wright, *Surprised by Hope: Rethinking Heaven, the Resurrection, and the Mission of the Church* (New York: HarperOne, 2008), 41.

32. Wright, *Surprised by Hope*, 151; emphasis in original.

33. Ehat and Cook, *Words of Joseph Smith*, 211, 213.

34. Josiah Quincy, *Figures of the Past* (Boston: Roberts Brothers, 1883), 391–92.

35. These are they who "were once enlightened, and have tasted of the heavenly gift, and were made partakers of the Holy Ghost, and have tasted the good word of God, and the powers of the world to come," who "crucify to themselves the Son of God afresh, and put him to an open shame," who have "trodden under foot the Son of God" and "done despite unto the Spirit of grace" (Hebrews 6:4–6; 10:29). They will at the time of death go into the postmortal spirit world and enter into that realm known as hell or outer darkness; they will eventually inherit a kingdom of no glory (see Doctrine and Covenants 88:24).

36. *Joseph Smith*, 224.

37. St. Augustine, *The City of God*, Modern Library Edition, trans. Marcus Dods (New York: Random House, 1978), 865; emphasis added.

38. Edwards, cited in Bruce Wilkinson, *A Life God Rewards: Why Everything You Do Today Matters Forever* (Sisters, OR: Multnomah Publishers, 2002), 119. Edwards's use of the word *designed* may well reflect his Calvinistic belief in predestination.

39. Wesley, "Notes on the Revelation of Jesus Christ," cited in Wilkinson, *A Life God Rewards*, 120–21.

40. Frederic W. Farrar, *The Early Days of Christianity* (New York: Cassell, Petter, Galpin & Co., 1882), 139–42, 169; emphasis added.

41. *Catechism of the Catholic Church*, part 1, article 5, paragraph 1, 180.
42. *Joseph Smith*, 408.
43. *Joseph Smith*, 471; emphasis added.
44. *Joseph Smith*, 471.

Chapter 8

THE CONDITION OF THE DEAD IN JEHOVAH'S WITNESS SOTERIOLOGY

Cary E. Valentine

Cary Valentine, a lifelong Jehovah's Witness, is a PhD candidate at Andrews University and adjunct faculty member at Baker University, where he teaches several topics related to organizational behavior and leadership.

I was born into a Jehovah's Witness family and reared to have faith in the beliefs and traditions of Jehovah God's organization. My father held leadership and ministerial duties within the local Kingdom Hall congregation, which our family attended several times each week. By 1975, my father was serving as the local presiding overseer,[1] which at that time was viewed by some as the weightiest of leadership roles in a local Witness congregation.[2] Still a relatively young man in his early thirties, my father managed a full plate of congregation duties (including administration of local field ministry activities, shepherding[3] of congregation members, preparing and delivering weekly meeting presentations, and working on several additional organization-related special projects), all performed without compensation.[4] Dad also juggled a full-time job working construction (during weekdays) and overseeing our family's needs in the evenings and weekends while at the same time fulfilling his ministerial duties. It was difficult balance to undertake and as a young boy, I could see the toll it took on him. Yet Dad felt it was what Jehovah God required of him in the last days of Satan's wicked system leading to the war of Armageddon as foretold in the bible book of Revelation 16:16. Dad was confident that his effort in serving zealously and tirelessly in the ministry would help facilitate his salvation as well those whom he led.

In 1975, the pressure on my father became even greater. At that time in organization's history, many of Jehovah's Witnesses speculated that the beginning of the seventh millennium of human existence would signify the end of the old-world system and beginning of Christ's rule.[5] The official history of Jehovah's Witnesses states: "During the years from 1935 through 1944, a review of the overall framework of Bible chronology . . . , along with certain other factors, . . . led to the idea—sometimes stated as a possibility, sometimes [stated] more firmly—that since the seventh millennium of human history would begin in 1975, events associated with the beginning of Christ's Millennial Reign might start to take place then."[6]

In 1975, I was nine years old and remember thinking that I could be a member of a generation that would never see death. Many others during this period held this same expectation of the potentiality of Christ's return—and the end of mortal death as we know it. Jehovah's Witnesses believe that there is a provision in God's plan of salvation whereby one can forgo the wages of sin through the ransom sacrifice of Jesus Christ and thereby never experience death. Thus, many Witnesses alive in 1975 expected that they would survive the pending war of Armageddon and then inherit a paradise-restored earth—having never tasted of death.[7] However, the expectations—held by *some* of Jehovah's Witnesses—regarding what would take place in 1975 were not met. Armageddon was *not* fought, and the resurrection of the dead to a paradise-restored earth did *not* happen. Many were terribly disappointed. Nevertheless, my interest in God's plan for salvation did not waver, nor did my father's, during this turbulent time. I had watched my paternal grandfather, who was also a faithful Witness of Jehovah, unexpectedly die when I was six years old. I remember seeing him for the final time, lying in an open casket, and hoping for that day when I would be reunited with him. I had every expectation that he would be resurrected in Jehovah God's restored earthly paradise. My father shared this same hope, fully expecting that he would see his father resurrected and dwelling in Jehovah's paradise-restored earth. Indeed, my father saved my grandfather's personal copy of the Bible with the intent of returning it to him on that glorious day.

While my father survived the 1975 disappointment spiritually unscathed and committed to the movement—including its doctrines on the afterlife—my mother's interest in Jehovah's Witnesses teachings wavered, along with the faith and commitment of many others whose expectations for 1975 went unfulfilled.[8] Within a couple of years after the expected date of Armageddon, my maternal grandmother, who served as a full-time Jehovah's Witness minister, suffered a fatal fall while working in the field ministry and died. After that, my mother was done being a Jehovah's Witness, citing among other reasons, a disagreement with Witness ideas regarding the status of dead.[9] Both as a child and as an adult, I often have found myself in the middle of my parent's forty-plus-year debate regarding God's plan of salvation and the Witness view on the state of the dead.

CONDITION OF THE SOUL AT DEATH?

For Jehovah's Witnesses, the "soul" is simply a term used to describe a creature that breathes or is a living being.[10] This reasoning is derived from the *New World Translation*'s rendering of the Hebrew word *nephesh* as a "creature" that breathes and the Greek word *psykhe*, traditionally interpreted as a "living being."[11] Unlike many in mainstream Christendom, Jehovah's Witnesses view the soul as the entire creature—not a separate part or spirit that is partitioned from the body and that can live outside of the body after death. In support of this view, Jehovah's Witnesses often reference Bible passages, such as Genesis 2:7, where it says of Adam that, upon creation, "man became a living soul."[12] This, to Witnesses, indicates that the "soul" is not distinct from the creature but, rather, *is the creature* it its entirety. Witnesses will also point to Ezekiel 18:4, 20, which states, "The soul that sinneth, it shall die," suggesting that the soul can die and thus represents the totality of the person rather than some separate spirit dwelling inside one's body.

Simply put, Jehovah's Witnesses hold the view that at death, a person ceases to exist. They argue that there is no limbo where the spirit or soul of the person goes to await the resurrection, no *immediate* visit to hell, purgatory, or heaven after a person dies.[13] Jehovah's Witnesses suggest that teachings contrary to this view are a product of apostate or otherwise non-Christian origin, ultimately designed to undermine the unselfish provisions Jehovah God has made available so that humans may live forever and never have to face death and the suffering that precedes it.[14]

Accordingly, Witnesses hold that no part of us lives on after we die; we are conscious of nothing once we enter the grave.[15] At death our brain stops working—our memories, feelings, and senses do not continue to function, and we do not—as individuals—survive the destruction of our brain. As one recent Witness publication noted: "The life we enjoy is like the flame of a candle. When the flame is put out, it does not *go* anywhere. It is simply gone."[16] At death you and I are simply gone because we have no "immortal soul or spirit." There is no "invisible part of the human" that "leaves the body and lives on" after we die. For Witnesses, there is no work accomplished by those whose bodies are in the grave. The dead do not suffer pain or heartache. They do not seek truth or connection with their loved ones. They cannot harm those of us who remain here upon the earth, and they do not need our help. In addition, we cannot speak with them and they cannot contact us. They simply don't exist.[17]

"Spirit" . . . refers to an invisible force (the spark of life) that animates all living creatures. . . . The body needs the spirit in much the same way as a radio needs electricity—in order to function. To illustrate this further, think of a portable radio. When you put batteries in a portable radio and turn it on, the electricity stored in the batteries brings the radio to life, so to speak. Without batteries, however, the radio is dead. So is another kind of radio when it is unplugged from an electric outlet. Similarly, the spirit is the force that brings our body to life. Also, like electricity, the spirit has no feeling and cannot think. It is an impersonal force. But without that spirit, or life-force, our bodies "expire, and back to their dust they go," as the psalmist stated. Speaking about man's death, Ecclesiastes 12:7 states: "The dust [of his body] returns to the earth just as it happened to be and the spirit itself returns to the true God who gave it." When the spirit, or life-force, leaves the body, the body dies and returns to where it came from—the earth. Comparably, the life-force returns to where it came from—God. (Job 34:14–15; Psalm 36:9) This does not mean that the life-force actually travels to heaven. Rather, it means that for someone who dies, any hope of future life rests with Jehovah God. His life is in God's hands, so to speak. Only by God's power can the spirit, or life-force, be given back so that a person may live again. . . . At the time of the resurrection, Jehovah will form a new body for a person sleeping in death and bring it to life by putting spirit, or life-force, in it.[18]

IS THERE A HELL?

Consistent with belief that the soul is not separate from the human creature and therefore dies with the person, Jehovah's Witnesses do not believe in an eternal place of punishment commonly referred to by most Christians as hell. Witnesses reject the idea that there is fiery hell put in place to eternally torment those deemed unrighteous at the time of death or afterwards.[19] Jehovah's Witnesses teach that the concept of an eternal place of torment stems from unscriptural origins, such as the teachings of the Greek philosopher Plato or the Catechism of the Catholic Church, each of which refers to such a place.[20] Witnesses believe that the rendering of the Hebrew word *Sheol*, typically translated as "hell" in various versions of the Bible, is a spuriously influenced concept better defined as the "common grave of mankind"—where all living creature activity, along with mental comprehension, ceases.[21]

According to Jehovah's Witnesses, it is unreasonable to assume that a loving God would destine humans to suffer horribly in eternal misery—as if having no life or consciousness isn't punishment enough. Witnesses argue that, as clarified in the case of Adam, "Dust you are and to dust you will return" (Genesis 3:19 New World Translation). This seems to suggest that the soul (or person) ceases awareness at the time of death—and thus teachings of hellfire are contrary to what is described in scripture and contrary to God's love for humankind.

Is there any distinction as to what happens to the faithful and rebellious at death? According to Witness teachings, those who (during their mortal lives) were practicing Witnesses of Jehovah, and those who knew *nothing* about Jehovah's truth and plan, will—upon death—sleep in Sheol or Hades, which is humankind's common grave. Witnesses believe that this is *not* a literal place. Rather, it is a "figurative location where most of mankind sleep in death." Those who knew the teachings of Jehovah and rejected them during their mortal lives will, on the other hand, be sent to Gehenna, which symbolizes complete and eternal destruction. Again, this is figurative, but it represents the post mortal status of those who will not be resurrected because they *knowingly* and *willfully* rejected the message of Jehovah's Witnesses when they heard it.[22] Thus, while Witnesses do not believe that anyone—wicked or righteous—continues to exist as a spirit/soul after they die, they do hold that there is a divine categorizing of people in anticipation of the coming resurrection.

WHAT IS HEAVEN?

Jehovah's Witnesses hold the view that the Bible delineates between three basic forms of heaven.[23] These include the physical heavens, a spirit realm, and a symbolic high or exalted place that is frequently referred to in scripture.

The "physical heavens" consist of the earth's atmosphere, where the weather forms and birds fly, yet it may also refer to outer space. This boundary of the physical heavens is described in Deuteronomy 4:19 (NWT), which states, "And when you raise your eyes to the heavens and see the sun and the moon and the stars—all the army of the heavens— do not get seduced and bow down to them and serve them. Jehovah your God has given them to all the peoples under the whole heavens." Jehovah God is not thought to dwell in the physical heavens. Even though the physical heavens can be viewed with the naked eye or with the assistance of telescopes capable of reaching far out into outer space, humans are constrained from seeing spirit creatures that might dwell in the physical heavens—except if they have taken on a facade comprehendible by humankind.[24]

Jehovah's Witnesses also acknowledge that, in scripture, the term "heaven" can also refer to a "spirit realm" which refers to a higher level or form of heaven over the physical heavens. In the spirit realm of heaven, Jehovah God (a spirit) resides—along with those faithful angels who make up the "congregation of the holy ones" described in Psalm 89:5–7 (NWT). Jehovah's Witnesses believe that Satan and his demons at one time may have been allowed to reside in this place. However, they were cast out, as described in Bible prophecy—though they have been allowed to continue their existence in spirit form. Jesus Christ is believed to have existed in the spirit realm before he came to earth to do the will of his Father.[25] To further clarify, the spirit realm form of heaven does not consist of matter or material that can be seen. In contrast to most of Christendom, Jehovah's Witnesses do not believe that the spirit realm is a place inhabited by multiple deities, ancestors of humans, or those mortal ones judged to have lived a good life by God while inhabiting the earth as humans.[26] There is also thought to be no communication (via mediums or any other means) by those who dwell in heaven with human souls. Indeed, those who attest to this type of communication were speculated in some Jehovah's Witness literature to mistakenly be communicating with lying spirits not in God's favor.[27]

The third part of Witness belief regarding heaven refers less to a location or venue of some sort but instead to a symbolic high place or elevated position typically associated with ruling authority.[28] Jehovah's Witnesses suggest that, in some scriptural passages, it is implied that heaven can be occupied by Jehovah God himself. His kingdom or government is prophesied to replace human rule, and a select remnant of Christian witnesses (144,000) hold a heavenly hope of ruling alongside him.[29]

As we will discuss below, in addition to these three forms or concepts of heaven per se, Witnesses also believe that this earth will become paradisiacal—and the ultimate abode of those who love Jehovah God and obey his commands.

TWO KINDS OF RESURRECTION

Jehovah's Witnesses describe the resurrection as a "rising up from death"—deriving this definition from the Greek word *anastasis*, meaning to raise or stand up.[30] God's ability to resurrect or restore human existence is established frequently in scripture, and is consistent with God's original purpose; namely that humankind would not experience death at all. Jehovah's Witnesses reason that God did *not* originally predestine humans to a certain life span or fate but instead gave humans the opportunity to choose to serve him or not.[31] Resurrection hope is available to those faithful ones who walked the earth before the coming of the Messiah and those who lived after him, along with those who perished in death without proper opportunity to accept the forgiveness of sin that Christ's ransom sacrifice makes possible. While Jehovah's Witnesses believe that the restored earth is the primary domain faithful humans will inhabit post-Armageddon, during the Millennium, and possibly beyond—scripture foretells of both an earthly and heavenly resurrection hope.

Jehovah's Witnesses view the "first resurrection," as mentioned in Revelation 20:4–6, to be the raising of those chosen to serve as kings and priests with Christ during the Millennium. Witnesses identify the number of this group, as mentioned in Revelation 14:1–4, literally to be 144,000. These individuals give up the natural hope of living forever on earth, though they originated as flesh-and-blood entities. Their ascension is thought to be immediate, meaning that at the time of death those chosen to be part of the first resurrection are instantaneously caught away to join the Lord within the spirit realm "in the blink of an eye" (1 Corinthians 15:51–52 NWT).

Jehovah's Witnesses also identify a second or earthly resurrection of both righteous *and* unrighteous individuals who have the potential to gain everlasting life on earth. Those deemed "righteous" but not appointed to serve with Christ in heaven (as part of the 144,000 or "anointed class") made use of the opportunity given them here on earth to learning of Jehovah God's plan and provision of the ransom sacrifice. These individuals repented, aligned their lives with God's principles, and served as Witnesses to those who had not yet heard the message of salvation God gifted to imperfect humans.

Jehovah's Witnesses believe that for some of those deemed unrighteous—but still resurrected in this second resurrection—there will be a resurrection of judgment. These individuals will still have an opportunity to gain eternal salvation during the Millennium. They will live as resurrected beings during the Millennium and, at its end, be judged by Christ and his 144,000 associates as either worthy of everlasting life or worthy of destruction. These are individuals who were in some way unable during mortality to learn of the life-saving provisions Jehovah had provided—either because they were not exposed to it during mortal life, or because they were otherwise unable to comprehend the message. Just as Adam was a perfect man choosing willingly to sin against Jehovah's law (while in Eden), so too will resurrected humans have a chance to make the choice to either serve God willingly or reject him and his plan. If they then follow Jehovah God at the end of Millennium, they will be restored to perfection.[32]

Jehovah's Witnesses hold that, at the end of Christ's Millennium, Satan will be released from his abyss to mislead and test human's resurrected to an earthly destiny. This will provide them with a choice to serve Jehovah God for the final time. Since humans will then be restored to a state of perfection, they will have the same simple choice Adam and Eve did at the time of creation—to serve God or to not. This Final Judgment involves those who reject Jehovah God and Christ's Jesus's ransom sacrifice and who will die a second time, never to be resurrected again. Indeed, they will cease to exist for eternity. At that time, the physical consequences of Adam's rebellion will no longer weigh humans down with the wages of sin, so the choice made to serve God or not is, as it was for Adam, one that is just, fair, and made of free will.

In summation, regarding the resurrection of the dead, Witnesses have a number of unique teachings.[33] First, as we alluded to earlier, Gehenna or the second death, is for those who had a "full knowledge of the truth" and yet rejected it, "choosing a course of opposition to God and righteousness."[34] They are the only ones who will not be resurrected. Once they have died, they cease to exist for eternity, whereas all others who have died cease to exist only temporarily.[35]

A second unique teaching of Jehovah's Witnesses regarding the resurrection has to do with the purpose of the Millennium. Witnesses hold "that there shall be a resurrection of the . . . just and unjust" (Acts 24:15), or the righteous and the unrighteous. Those who accepted the Witness message and lived it during mortality (i.e., the "righteous" or "just") and those who never had a chance to hear it or understand it (i.e., the "unjust" or "unrighteous"[36]) will be resurrected during the Millennium and will have a *chance* to live forever—though not all resurrected beings will live forever.[37] If those who had not heard the message during mortality reject it during the Millennium, they will die a second time and will then cease to exist throughout eternity. Thus, according to Witness belief, those resurrected to the earth at the beginning of the thousand-year reign of Christ, *can* in fact, die a second time when in the state of perfection.[38]

Finally, Witnesses also hold that there will be a physical resurrection and a spiritual one.[39] The 144,000—or "spirit-anointed Christians"—will be resurrected as spirits. For these chosen few, their spirit resurrection is thought to be instantaneous upon their death.[40] Those faithful ones who are not part of the 144,000 are thought to be destined to live upon the earth in paradise forever. This group will enjoy a physical resurrection during the Millennium and are anticipated to have their personality and all their memories and beliefs completely restored.

While all Christian denominations have certain elements of their soteriology that may be unique to them, Witness teachings about salvation are perhaps the most unique and certainly the most prone to misunderstanding.

NOTES

1. Effective 1 January 2009, Jehovah's Witnesses ceased to use the term "presiding overseer," replacing the title with "coordinator of the body of elders." See "Announcements," *Our Kingdom Ministry*, 8 November 2008, 3.

2. It has been the practice of Jehovah's Witnesses in the past several decades to refrain from isolating authority to individual members of the congregation elder body.

3. The term "shepherding" refers to an activity where congregation elders and ministerial servants visit those in the congregation in need of spiritual counsel, be it consoling or admonishment in some cases. See "They Compassionately Shepherd the Little Sheep," *The Watchtower*, 15 September 1993, 20–21.

4. Those who serve in leadership roles within Jehovah's Witness Kingdom Halls do not receive compensation.

5. See "Why Are You Looking Forward to 1975?," *The Watchtower*, 15 August 1968, 494–95. See also *Jehovah's Witnesses: Proclaimers of God's Kingdom* (Brooklyn, NY: Watchtower Bible and Tract Society of Pennsylvania, 1993), 633. The year 1975 was predicted in 1966 as a "date of significance," though

what exactly should be expected was left somewhat vague. Many Witnesses, including some on the Governing Body (i.e., the Jehovah's Witnesses' highest quorum of leadership), believed that 1975 would be the conclusion of Armageddon, the binding of Satan, and the beginning of the Millennium and Christ's thousand-year reign. Again, the leaders of the Society highlighted the date but were not specific as to what exactly they were predicting would happen on that date. See *Jehovah's Witnesses: Proclaimers of God's Kingdom*, 104. The most explicit statement on what was expected to take place in 1975 is found in the 1966 Witness publication entitled *Life Everlasting in Freedom of the Sons of God*, which states that "six thousand years from man's creation will end in 1975, and the seventh period of a thousand years of human history will begin in the fall of 1975 CE. So, six thousand years of man's existence on earth will soon be up, yes, within this generation.... So, in not many years [approximately nine]... we are reaching what Jehovah God could view as the seventh day of man's existence. How appropriate it would be for Jehovah God to make of this coming seventh period of a thousand years: ... the reign of Jesus Christ over the earth for a thousand years, the millennial reign of Christ." *Life Everlasting in Freedom of the Sons of God* (Brooklyn, NY: Watchtower Bible and Tract Society of New York, 1966), 29–30.

6. *Jehovah's Witnesses: Proclaimers of God's Kingdom*, 632–33.

7. See "What Is the Best Gift of All?," *The Watchtower*, public edition, 2017, no. 6, 6–7.

8. As an example of how the Society's leadership felt about their predictions, and how the average lay Witnesses believed their leader's interpretations of Bible chronology, note what the May 1974 issue of the monthly Witnesses paper (entitled *Kingdom Ministry*) stated, "Reports are heard of brothers selling their homes and property and planning to finish out the rest of their days in this old system in the pioneer service. Certainly, this is a fine way to spend the short time remaining before the wicked world's end." "How Are You Using Your Life?" *Kingdom Ministry*, May 1974, 3. In reality, a number of Witnesses *did* sell their homes or quit their jobs in anticipation of the "world's end"—and with the intent of focusing all of their time and efforts on preaching the word until the "end" actually arrived. Some Witnesses postponed needed healthcare, while others liquidated any assets they had— again, in order to have the cash to live off of so that they could spend the

remaining days in full-time preaching of Jehovah's word. However, when 1975 passed with nothing of significance happening, some became disillusioned; others simply picked up the pieces and moved forward, trusting that God's will would be done when he felt it was time. Some do not feel that this event caused any great disappointment or disillusionment among faithful Witnesses. However others, like my mother, found it devastating and left the movement. Clearly, different people responded in different ways. Regardless, this was a difficult time for Jehovah's Witnesses—and, for some, this remains a frustrating era in the organization's history.

9. This put considerable strain on my parents' marriage and within three years of 1975 they divorced, and my father was forced to relinquish his leadership roles in the congregation.

10. See "What Is the Soul?," https://www.jw.org/en/bible-teachings/questions /what-is-a-soul/.

11. See "Soul," *Insight on the Scriptures* (Brooklyn, NY: Watchtower Bible and Tract Society of New York, 1988), 2:1004.

12. Biblical passages are cited from the King James Version unless otherwise noted.

13. See "Where or What Is Limbo?," *The Watchtower*, 15 September 1988.

14. See "Myth 1: The Soul Is Immortal," *The Watchtower*, 1 November 2009.

15. See *Jehovah's Witnesses: Proclaimers of God's Kingdom*, 70, 127, 145, 156.

16. See *What Does the Bible Really Teach?* (Wallkill, NY: Watchtower Bible and Tract Society of New York, 2006), 58–59.

17. *What Does the Bible Really Teach?*, 58, 64, 208.

18. *What Does the Bible Really Teach?*, 210–11.

19. See "Myth 2: The Wicked Suffer in Hell," *The Watchtower*, 1 November 2009.

20. See "What Is Hell? Is It a Place of Eternal Torment?" https://www.jw.org /en/bible.teachings/questions/what-is-hell/.

21. See "*What Does the Bible Really Teach?*" (Wallkill, NY: Watchtower Bible and Tract Society of New York, 2014), appendix.

22. See "Gehenna," in *Insight on the Scriptures*, 1:905–6; "Sheol," in *Insight on the Scriptures*, 2:922–23; *What Does the Bible Really Teach?* (2006), 212–13. Witnesses note that only God can judge. If someone is sent to Gehenna, it was because they were judged by God to be "wicked" in heart. Witnesses stress that some reject the Witness message for reasons other than

wickedness (e.g., misunderstandings, prejudice, or preoccupations). These will not be sent to Gehenna, and many will eventually accept the message of the Witnesses.

23. See "Who Go to Heaven?," https://www.jw.org/en/bible-teachings/questions/go-to-heaven/.

24. Jehovah's Witnesses reason that, unlike spirit creatures, humans consist of flesh and blood. Thus, humans do not possess the same sensory abilities that spirit creatures possess and can't comprehend certain types of phenomena spirit creatures are able to experience and comprehend.

25. See "Questions About Those in the Spirit Realm," *The Watchtower*, public edition, 2016, no. 6.

26. "Who Go to Heaven?"

27. *Can You Talk with the Dead? Is This Life All There Is?* (Wallkill, NY: Watchtower Bible and Tract Society of New York, 1981), 74–78.

28. "Heaven," *Awake!*, 2016, no. 1, 14–15.

29. "God's Judgment Makes Manifest the Truly Rich," *The Watchtower*, 1 April 1967, 212–19. In some scriptural instances, "heaven" has reference to human governments who have exalted themselves unjustly—or to those wicked spirits who seek to propagate evil in the world, but who will soon face destruction. In years past, Jehovah's Witness literature often stated that the "present system of things"—along with the symbolic heaven—will be "shaken," removing all creatures at enmity with God's purpose and kingdom.

30. See *Insight on the Scriptures*, 2:783–93.

31. Jehovah God purposed that Adam and Eve would multiply and fill the earth with humankind, and that has not changed. If God's purpose is perfect, then there is no need for it to be altered, and in fact it must be fulfilled as he planned.

32. "A Grand Millennium Approaching," *The Watchtower*, 1 June 1990, 5–7.

33. See "Resurrection," in *Insight on the Scriptures*, 2:783–93.

34. See *Jehovah's Witnesses: Proclaimers of God's Kingdom*, 129; "Resurrection," in *Insight on the Scriptures*, 2:791–92.

35. See *What Does the Bible Really Teach?* (2006), 73.

36. See "Resurrection," 2:788; *What Does the Bible Really Teach?* (2006), 72–73.

37. See *What Does the Bible Really Teach?* (2006), 36.

38. See *What Does the Bible Really Teach?* (2006), 70. A friend of mine, who is an elder in a Utah Witness congregation, has used the following analogy:

"If a Hindu living in India had never had a chance to know about Jehovah's Witnesses and their message, at death he would 'sleep' (in the grave). Then, during the Millennium, this Hindu would come forth as a resurrected being and get his chance to accept true Christianity. At that point, if this Hindu rejected the Witness message, he would die a second time and then cease (from that point forward) to exist in any form or capacity. If, on the other hand, the Hindu from India accepted the message of the Witnesses (as presented to him as a resurrected being during the Millennium), he would be blessed to live in paradise on earth forever (now as a true Christian, rather than as a Hindu). But, on the other hand, if he had studied with the Witnesses during mortality and did not accept the message they bear, then upon death he would simply sleep forever—as he had had his 'chance.'" I should add that all good Witnesses will tell you that only Jehovah God knows who *really* has or has not had his or her "chance." Thus, Witnesses avoid judging people. They simply explain how they understand things will play out after one dies.

39. See "Resurrection," 2:787–88; *What Does the Bible* Really *Teach?* (2006), 71, 73–74.

40. See *What Does the Bible* Really *Teach?* (2006), 74.

Chapter 9

WAKING UP TO ETERNITY

Ella Smith Simmons

Ella Smith Simmons, a Seventh-day Adventist scholar, is general vice president of the Seventh-day Adventist World Church in Silver Spring, Maryland.

INTRODUCTION

My brother-in-law, Ralph, nicknamed Cowboy, died in 2014. Ralph had been a horseman and avid roller skater practically up to the end. From as early as they could walk, he took his children and grandchildren to the roller rink for his favorite form of physical exercise. They loved him for it and participated with him in his skating enthusiasm throughout the varying stages of their own lives. Then at his funeral, as they sobbed quietly and comforted each other in their loss with embraces, strained smiles, and understanding nods, as is often the case, the eulogist proclaimed the familiar sentiment: "Ralph is up in heaven now looking down on us." The eulogist said, "I can just see him now, not walking, but skating all over heaven, up and down the streets of gold!" Most of the family, especially Ralph's children and grandchildren, found comfort and rejoiced in that thought.

In his article "Waking Up to Eternity," from which the title for this paper is taken, Philip Rodonioff says regarding the funeral for his grand-mother, his first funeral: "I was just a child and what remained in my memory was the sadness, the cloudy emotions, and the 'grayness' of it all. Later, as a medical doctor, I encountered death more frequently, but I never became accustomed to it."[1]

Niels-Erik Andreasen wrote, "Like an unwelcome guest making frequent calls, death walks boldly into our families to claim our loved ones."[2] John Dybdahl added: "All of us have an interest in the topic of death, because we all face it in our future until the Second Coming of Christ. But what is death? What happens to people when they die? Are people conscious in death? Where do immortality and everlasting life come into a person's life? Can the dead communicate with the living? Is the grave the ultimate end? These and other questions have been of special interest from the dawn of history because they have eternal con-sequences."[3] Scripture, Genesis to Revelation, addresses this quest for understanding (Genesis 2:7; Psalms 6:5; 115:17; 146:4; Ecclesiastes 9:5; 12:7; Daniel 12:2; John 5:28–29; 11:11, 26; Acts 7:60; Romans 6:23; 1 Corinthians 15:51–55; 1 Thessalonians 4:13; Revelation 20:14).[4]

The challenge in the Garden of Eden that resulted in the fall of humankind was on this key understanding. What does it mean to die? By the time of the early church, two conflicting understandings of death had emerged, each responding to the problem of death in a different way: the biblical or Hebrew understanding of death as the sure end of life, which can be restored only by a new re-creative act of God, and the Greek understanding of death as the beginning of new life, with its affirmation of the soul's continued existence after separation from the body at death. Cullmann explained this difference dramatically in his illustrative contrast between the ways Jesus and Socrates faced the expe-rience of dying.[5] As illustrated by the experience of Jesus, the Bible pres-ents death as a foe, the enemy of God, and the destroyer of life. On the other hand, as illustrated by the experience of Socrates, Greek thought portrays death as a welcome friend, releasing a soul long imprisoned in the body into a new life of the spirit.

ANTHROPOLOGICAL CONTEXT

In the introduction to the book *What Are Human Beings That You Are Mindful of Them?*, Artur Stele poses the essential questions for a study of life after death: What are human beings? Who am I? Where do I come from? Where am I going? He says, "These are questions that confront us all and which biblical anthropology seeks to answer."[6] He sets the foundation for anthropological underpinnings in scripture and asserts that the passage in "Genesis 1:26 and 27 has been widely regarded as the key proposition of biblical anthropology."[7]

Stele warns that it may also be fruitful to explore the connection between anthropological dualism and spiritualism in its diversity of expressions. He queries: To what extent have these two perspectives been connected throughout the history of ideas? Has there been a connection between demonology in dualism? He acknowledges, "Currently much emphasis is being placed on discoveries about the human body, including insights from microbiology and epigenetics, as making important contributions to our understanding of human existence. It seems that in recent discussions within philosophical anthropology the body as an essential substratum for human existence has been rediscovered."[8]

Stele then notes, "Biblical anthropology is a very broad field of study and quite a difficult one, because it relates to almost every other major biblical teaching. To understand biblical anthropology requires an understanding, first of all, of the doctrine of Creation, as well as of hamartiology, soteriology, eschatology, and even ecclesiology."[9] He cites eschatology as of special interest to Seventh-day Adventists and notes that concerning contemporary views of life after death, "It is here, in connection with the biblical view of human destiny, of death and resurrection, that we can make significant contributions."[10]

Whalen, reflecting on Burnet's work on the concept of soul, shows that "beginning with Homer, Greek literature provides a wealth of speculation regarding the nature of human beings, death, and the afterlife. The earliest Greek conceptions of which we can be sure identify the human "soul" (psyche) with the breath that the dying person struggles to retain until at last the "ghost" is given up."[11] He examines also Hebrew perspectives and, quoting James Arieti from "The Vocabulary of Septuagint Amos,"[12] points out, "When the Septuagint refers to the soul of a person it comprehends the whole being or life of the person and cannot be construed in terms of a bipartite (body-soul) or tripartite (body-soul-spirit) concept of human nature."[13]

HISTORICAL BACKGROUND

Andreasen notes, "The contrast between the classical (Greek) understanding and the biblical (Hebrew) of death is profound."[14] Following is a discussion of differences.

GREEK VIEW

Prior to the emergence of the philosophers, in the time of Homer (ninth century BC), the Greeks believed that death brought an end to consciousness and thought, leaving only a bodiless, shadowy, unconscious "existence" (*Iliad* 23:69–107; *Odyssey* 11:204–23).[15] In mythology, for example, the hero Orpheus tells of his attempt to achieve a release for his wife from the underworld. The beliefs and assumptions are apparent that something of the individual continues to live after the death of the body.

Other ancient stories equally demonstrate the progression of thought on the afterlife. "By the time of Socrates (470–399 B.C.) and Plato (427–347 B.C.) soul immortality came to clear expression in public discourse, as illustrated, for example, in the *Phaedo*, which records the last hours of Socrates's life. Socrates expressed his belief that at death the soul is freed from the impure body to live on independently, released from the corporeal."[16] Although Aristotle, Lucretius, and others challenged Plato's idea of an entity called a soul that was separate from the person or body, to this day Socrates's and Plato's theories of a continually existent soul separate from the body are reflected in a wide variety of worldviews.

From the earliest times, these views were considered comforting to those who had lost loved ones in death and assuring to those who faced it. It has been found in Hebrew literature that although from scripture they had a different perspectival foundation, Jewish people also entertained a view of a separately existing and immortal soul. "For example, 2 Maccabees 6:30 reports the death of pious Eleazer with these words: 'I am enduring terrible sufferings in my body under this beating, but in my soul I am glad to suffer these things because I fear him.' Another example is 2 Maccabees 12:43–45 which describes a sin offering of 2,000 silver drachmas for the purpose of making atonement for the dead."[17]

HEBREW VIEW

The Old Testament root word for death and dying (*mwt*) occurs one thousand times in the Hebrew Bible in its various derivative forms.[18] The words for death all indicate the termination of life and all of its functions. In Acts 28:6 and Romans 7:8, the language for dead indicates a state of lifelessness, the opposite of being alive, as in Mark 12:27: "Probably the best explanation of death from a Hebrew standpoint is simply to describe it as the reversal of God's creation of human beings."[19]

The preponderance of biblical perspective on death is summed up in its characterization of death as a sleep (Deuteronomy 31:16; 1 Kings 2:10; Job 14:12; Daniel 12:2; Matthew 9:24; 27:51, 52; John 11:11; Acts 7:60; 1 Corinthian 15:18, 51; 1 Thessalonians 4:13). "The symbol of sleep illustrates well both the biblical understanding of death and its concept of resurrection, an event similar to an awakening (1 Thessalonians 4:15–18)."[20]

The Bible favors the metaphor of sleep to describe the condition in death (Deuteronomy 31:16; 1 Kings 2:10; Job 14:12; Daniel 12:2; Matthew 9:24; 27:51–52; John 11:11; Acts 7:60; 1 Corinthians 15:18, 51; 1 Thessalonians 4:13). In his exhaustive study of the sixty-six uses of the term Sheol in Hebrew Bible, Eriks Galenieks found no support for the association of the term with an after-death experience or an underworld in which the dead are conscious. Rather, he demonstrated the opposite.[21] Genesis 3:19 is clear in reference back to chapter 2, verse 7 as it says, "In the sweat of your face you shall eat bread; Till you return to the ground, For out of it you were taken; For dust you *are*, And to dust you shall return."[22]

Yet, while the biblical view of death as an unconscious state (sleep) awaiting the resurrection continued in the early church, over time the apparently incompatible views became blended in Christian teachings on life, death, the soul, an intermediate state, resurrection, and the final judgment.[23] These amalgamations continue to this day. In fact, it appears that "the majority of Christian traditions, as well as non-Christian religions, believe strongly in the immortality of the human soul."[24]

While for this treatment we draw rather discrete lines of distinction, in reality the lines are not as clear. Note Ruppert's conclusions from his assessment of various views on the topic of life after death. He says, focusing here on Seventh-day Adventist beliefs:

> While there are several verses that would indicate that there is no consciousness after death (Eccl 9:5–6, 10; Ps 6:5), Jesus clearly taught that there is a distinction between body and soul. "And do not fear those who kill the body but cannot kill the soul. But rather fear Him who is able to destroy both soul and body in hell" (Matt 10:28). . . . Anyone can kill another person's body but his soul is not killed. . . . John also spoke of both body and soul as being two parts of our being. "Beloved, I pray that you may prosper in all things and be in health, just as your soul prospers" (3 John 2). The implication

is obvious that our body may or may not be healthy but our souls can prosper regardless of what is happening to our body. . . . The writer[s] of Hebrews, James, and Peter imply that our souls are a separate part of us destined for eternity (Heb 13:17, James 1:21, 5:20; 1 Peter 1:9).[25]

SEVENTH-DAY ADVENTIST PERSPECTIVES

Nevertheless, in contrast to the belief in an inherently immortal soul that exists independently of the body, Seventh-day Adventists believe that scripture emphasizes repeatedly that the human person, or soul, is one whole unit of physical body and spirit, and that ceases at death. These beliefs are foundational to many related concepts of the state of the dead. Seventh-day Adventist understandings on human nature, death, and the resurrection compose one interrelated system of knowledge.

First, interpretations of scripture that determine Seventh-day Adventist beliefs on death include the following underlying principles:

1. Only God is innately immortal (1 Timothy 6:16).
2. Immortality is a gift from God to the saved (1 Thessalonians 4:16).
3. Death is a sleep until Christ returns (1 Thessalonians 4:13–15; 1 Corinthians 15:6, 18, 20).[26]

The Seventh-day Adventist Church expresses its foundational beliefs in the *Twenty-eight Fundamental Beliefs of the Seventh-day Adventist Church*. These beliefs constitute the church's understanding and expression of the teachings of scripture. Among these are specific beliefs about death and resurrection that are fundamentals to the Seventh-day Adventist faith base.

For this discussion, we consider two of the fundamentals, although to achieve a full understanding of Seventh-day Adventist beliefs one should study all twenty-eight for context and interrelatedness. However, present space will not permit that study.

The first for this discussion is the Seventh-day Adventist Church's Fundamental Belief 7, "The Nature of Humanity":

> Man and woman were made in the image of God with individuality, the power and freedom to think and to do. Though created free beings, each is an indivisible unity of body, mind, and spirit, dependent upon God for life and breath and all else. When our first parents disobeyed God, they denied their dependence upon Him and fell from their high position. The image of God in them was marred and they became subject to death. Their descendants share this fallen nature and its consequences. They are born with weaknesses and tendencies to evil. But God in Christ reconciled the world to Himself and by His Spirit restores in penitent mortals the image of their Maker. Created for the glory of God, they are called to love Him and one another, and to care for their environment.[27]

The key concept in this belief statement is that each human being was created as an indivisible unity of body, mind, and spirit, dependent upon God for life and breath and all else. This belief emerges from an understanding of the following biblical passages within the broader context of scripture (Genesis 1:26–28; 2:7, 15, 3; Psalms 8:4–8; 51:5, 10; 58:3; Jeremiah 17:9; Acts 17:24–28; Romans 5:12–17; 2 Corinthians 5:19, 20; Ephesians 2:3; 1 Thessalonians 5:23; 1 John 3:4; 4:7–8, 11, 20).

From his research in theological anthropology, LeRon Shults observes, "In the last two centuries, biblical scholars have increasingly moved toward a consensus that both the Hebrew Bible and the New Testament provide a holistic model of the human person."[28] Richard Davidson goes to the creation account in his alignment with this view. In his claims on the constitution of the human being, Davidson declares, "A virtual consensus within biblical scholarship considers the opening chapters of Genesis as foundational for the rest of the canon,"[29] and quotes John Rankin, "'Whether one is evangelical or liberal, it is clear that Genesis 1–3 is the interpretive foundation of all Scripture.'"[30]

"Genesis 1," he asserts, "presents humanity as created in the image of God (imago Dei), while the constitution of humans is set forth in

Genesis 2."[31] Genesis 1 says: "In the beginning God created the heavens and the earth. . . . Then God said, "Let Us make man in Our image, according to Our likeness. . . . So God created man in His *own* image; in the image of God He created him; male and female He created them" (Genesis 1:1, 26–27).[32] Genesis 2 states, "And the Lord God formed man *of* the dust of the ground, and breathed into his nostrils the breath of life; and man became a living being" (Genesis 2:7).

Davidson acknowledges, "It has become increasingly apparent that Genesis 2:7 (like 1:26) articulates a wholistic view of the human being; [that] he/she does not *have* a soul, but *is* a soul, a psychophysical unity. Genesis 2:7 gives the basic 'formula' for the constitution of humans: 'dust' + 'breath of life' = 'soul.'"[33] Genesis 2:7 says, "Then the Lord God formed man of dust from the ground, and breathed into his nostrils the breath of life; and man became a living being" (Gen. 2:7). So, again, the schematic formula for human life is: dust of the ground *('āpār min hā 'ǂdāmāh)* + breath of life *(nišmaṯ ḥayyim)* = living being *(nepeš ḥayyāh).*[34]

In the Flood narrative, the phrase "breath of life" in Genesis 2:7 is equivalent to "spirit of life" or the longer form, "breath of the spirit of life" (Genesis 6:17; 7:22).[35] (We also say heart when we mean mind.) The presentation in Genesis 2:7 makes clear that the breath is not a conscious entity within the human being, but rather it is the "animating 'life principle' or 'vital power' bestowed by God on living beings."[36] Of the 378 times the term refers to humans in the Old Testament, it is used in regard to human dynamic vitality.[37]

The Hebrew word for "being" means life or person, not an eternal separate entity. The Bible is consistent in its discussion of life and death. If life came when God formed humans from the elements of the earth and breathed life into them, death is described as the exact opposite. Ecclesiastes 12:7 says, "Then [at the point of death] the dust will return to the earth as it was, and the spirit will return to God who gave it." Death unravels the association of God's breath or spirit with the elements of the earth, and the person as living being ceases to exist (see Psalm 115:17; 146:4; Daniel 12:2; John 11:11–14; 1 Thessalonians 4:13–14).[38]

In Genesis 2:7 the Hebrew word used 754 times in the Old Testament and translated as "person," "being," or "individual" consistently never refers to an "indestructible core of being" that lives beyond the physical being. Davidson notes, "Since the early 1950s and the rise of the biblical theology movement, this view has become the standard interpretation, leaving no room for a platonic/philonic dichotomy of body and soul. Rather, the picture of the constitution of humans throughout the Hebrew Bible is one of wholism."[39]

Francis Nichol observes, "The word 'to form,' *yaṣar*, implies an act of molding and fashioning into a form corresponding in design and appearance to the divine plan. The word is used in describing the activity of the potter (Isa. 29:16; 49:5; etc.), of the goldsmith fashioning idols (Isa. 44:9; Hab. 2:18), and of God, who fashions various things, among others, the light (Isa. 45:7)."[40]

God did not simply speak man and woman into existence but rather formed each of them using his hands, as it were, and man (Hebrew *'adam*) is created from the dust of the earth (Hebrew *'adamah*) and not from divine matter as in other contemporary creation accounts. He will return to dust when he dies (Genesis 3:19).[41]

> From the Source of all life the life-giving principle [breath, or *neshamah*] entered the lifeless body of Adam. The agency by which the spark of life was transferred to his body is said to be the "breath" of God. The same thought appears in Job 33:4, "The breath [*neshamah*] of the almighty hath given me life." Imparted to man, the "breath" is equivalent to his life; it is life itself (Isa. 2:22). At death there is "no breath [*neshamah*, life] left in him" (1 Kings 17:17). . . .
>
> When the lifeless form of man was infused with this divine "breath," *neshamah*, of life, man became a living "soul," *nephesh*. The word *nephesh* has a variety of meanings: (1) breath (Job 41:21), (2) life (1 Kings 17:21; 2 Sam. 18:13; etc.), (3) heart as the seat of

affections (Gen. 34:3; S of Sol. 1:7; etc.), [and] (4) living being (Genesis 12:5; 36:6; Lev. 4:2; etc.). . . . Note that the *nephesh* is made by God (Jer. 38:16), and can die (Judges 16:30), be killed (Num. 31:19), be eaten (metaphorically, Eze. 22:25), be redeemed (Ps. 34:22), and be refreshed (Ps. 19:7, Heb.). None of this applies to the spirit, *ruach*, indicating clearly the great difference between the two terms. This passage may rightly be translated: "Man became a living being" (RSV). When "soul" is considered synonymous with "being," we gain the Scriptural meaning of *nephesh* in this text.[42]

Next consider the Seventh-day Adventist Fundamental Belief 26, *Death and Resurrection*. It declares:

> The wages of sin is death. But God, who alone is immortal, will grant eternal life to His redeemed. Until that day death is an unconscious state for all people. When Christ, who is our life, appears, the resurrected righteous and the living righteous will be glorified and caught up to meet their Lord. The second resurrection, the resurrection of the unrighteous, will take place a thousand years later.

The core of Seventh-day Adventist belief on this topic is that *death is an unconscious state for all people who will be resurrected when Christ appears at the Second Coming.* This belief emerges from an understanding of the following biblical passages within the broader context of scripture (Job 19:25–2; Psalm 146:3–4; Ecclesiastes 9:5, 6, 10; Daniel 12:2, 13; Isaiah 25:8; John 5:28–29; 11:11–14; Romans 6:23; 16; 1 Corinthians 15:51–54; Colossians 3:4; 1 Thessalonians 4:13–17; 1 Timothy 6:15; Revelation 20:1–10).[43]

STATE OF THE DEAD

Ignatius of Antioch (ca. AD 107) wrote, "Labour together with one another; strive in company together, run together, suffer together, sleep together [in death], and awake together [in the resurrection], as stewards, and associates, and servants of God."[44]

The dead know nothing (Ecclesiastes 9:5). They cannot talk or praise God (Psalms 6:5; 88:11; 115:17), their thinking and planning have ceased (Psalm 146:4), they do not sense God's presence (Job 7:21), and they have no hope (Isaiah 38:18).[45] Andreasen writes, "At death all ordinary life processes as we know them cease. In death work, and thus rewards, cease (Eccl. 9:5). Love, hate, and envy perish, along with participation in life's events (verse 6). Thought, knowledge, and wisdom no longer exist (verses 5, 10). The dead cannot lay plans (Ps. 146:4), and there is neither remembrance of the dead (Ps. 6:5; Eccl. 9:5) nor praise of God after death (Ps. 88:10, 11; 115:17; Isa. 38:18). The dead remain in the grave (Acts 2:29, 34)." He adds, "Biblical descriptions portray the experience of dying as slipping into an unconscious state in which all normal mental functions such as thinking, planning, loving, hoping, and believing cease"[46] (compare Ecclesiastes 9:5, 6, 10; Psalm 88:3–7).

Scripture does not teach that the righteous go to their reward or the wicked to their punishment immediately at death. Andreasen notes that the dead "are represented as sleeping until the resurrection (1 Thess. 4:14; Job 14:10–12). In the very day when the silver cord is loosed and the golden bowl broken (Eccl. 12:6), man's thoughts perish. They that go down to the grave are in silence. They know no more of anything that is done under the sun (Job 14:21)."[47] He adds, "Time, be it long or short, is but a moment to them. They sleep; they are awakened by the trump of God to a glorious immortality. 'For the trumpet shall sound, and the dead shall be raised incorruptible. So when this corruptible shall have put on incorruption, and this mortal shall have put on immortality, then shall be brought to pass the saying that is written, Death is swallowed up in victory' (1 Corinthians 15:52–54)."[48]

THE RESURRECTION

Andreasen writes, "No one, whether saint or sinner, receives the final reward, salvation or damnation, at death. That must await the resurrection.

'For the hour is coming when all who are in the tombs will hear his voice and come forth, those who have done good, to the resurrection of life, and those who have done evil, to the resurrection of judgment (John 5:28, 29; cf. Dan. 12:2).' Death does indeed seal everyone's fate according to what was done in life, but the dead themselves are unconscious of any human activities, as in sleep, awaiting the resurrection, the judgment, and their respective rewards (2 Cor. 5:1–4, 10; Heb. 9:27)."[49]

All matters associated with eternal life or death must therefore follow the resurrection, either the resurrection unto life—leading to an imperishable body, immortality (1 Corinthians 15:52–54), and the eternal presence of God (1 Thessalonians 4:17) for God's Saints—or the resurrection unto death—bringing destruction and eternal obliteration for those who have rejected the salvation of God (Matthew 25:31–46; Revelation 20).[50]

The resurrection hope is firmly established in both the Gospels and the Epistles (Matthew 22:31, 32; Luke 20:27–38; John 11:24; 1 Corinthians 15:51–53; 1 Thessalonians 4:13–18; Hebrews 11:19). "Jesus gave advanced assurance of this hope by raising the dead to life (Matt. 9:23–25; Luke 7:11–17; John 11:38–44), an assurance God affirmed by raising Christ from the dead, whereby all believers may enjoy eternal life (John 3:16; 5:25–29; 6:39, 40; 1 Cor. 15:20–23; 1 Peter 1:3; 1 Cor. 15:51–53; 1 Thess. 4:13–18)."[51]

THE ERADICATION OF DEATH THROUGH THE RESURRECTION

Andreasen writes, "Following the resurrection, God's gift of eternal life to all who believe in Christ will signify the end of the power of death and break its dominion over humankind (2 Tim. 1:8–10). Christ accomplished this through His own death and resurrection: 'For we know that Christ being raised from the dead will never die again; death no longer has dominion over him' (Rom. 6:9; cf. Rev. 1:18). A resurrection, unlike a resuscitation, does not cheat death of its power in the last minute but effectively breaks the power of death. Hence 'death no longer has dominion over him' (Rom. 6:9)."[52]

A wonderfully animated illustration of the resurrection is found in Ezekiel 37:1–14:

> The hand of the LORD came upon me and brought me out in the Spirit of the LORD, and set me down in the midst of the valley; and it *was* full of bones. Then He caused me to pass by them all around, and behold, *there were* very many in the open valley; and indeed *they were* very dry. And He said to me, "Son of man, can these bones live?"
>
> So I answered, "O Lord GOD, You know." Again He said to me, "Prophesy to these bones, and say to them, 'O dry bones, hear the word of the LORD!'" Thus says the Lord GOD to these bones: "Surely I will cause breath to enter into you, and you shall live. I will put sinews on you and bring flesh upon you, cover you with skin and put breath in you; and you shall live. Then you shall know that I *am* the LORD."
>
> So I prophesied as I was commanded; and as I prophesied, there was a noise, and suddenly a rattling; and the bones came together, bone to bone. Indeed, as I looked, the sinews and the flesh came upon them, and the skin covered them over; but *there was* no breath in them.
>
> Also He said to me, "Prophesy to the breath, prophesy, son of man, and say to the breath, 'Thus says the Lord GOD: "Come from the four winds, O breath, and breathe on these slain, that they may live."'" So I prophesied as He commanded me, and breath came into them, and they lived, and stood upon their feet, an exceedingly great army.
>
> Then He said to me, "Son of man, these bones are the whole house of Israel. They indeed say, 'Our bones are dry, our hope is lost, and we ourselves are cut off!' Therefore prophesy and say to them, 'Thus says the Lord GOD: "Behold, O My people, I will open your graves and cause you to come up from your graves, and bring you into the land of Israel. Then you shall know that I *am* the LORD, when I have opened your graves, O My people, and brought you up

from your graves. I will put My Spirit in you, and you shall live, and I will place you in your own land. Then you shall know that I, the LORD, have spoken *it* and performed *it*," says the LORD.'"

Ezekiel's third vision (Ezekiel 37:1–14) depicts a resurrected nation. God's word and breath (Spirit) bring life back into the dead dry bones (37:4–5). Dybdahl writes, "It is the imagery about God who will resurrect the dead, exiled nation (v. 11) from the grave into life, giving them their land (v. 12), and a new spiritual life through His word and Spirit (vv. 12, 14; Titus 3:4–6)."[53] This illustration is a vivid portrayal of restoration of the individual in the resurrection as well. Kwabena Donkor summarizes:

> The Bible teaches that in the resurrection God restores the body to life (Rom. 8:11; Phil. 3:20, 21). In other words, biblical resurrection is a bodily resurrection. Remember that when Christ was resurrected, the tomb was empty. But biblical resurrection is not the result of an eternal immortal soul reuniting with the new, physical body. In the Bible the word translated "soul" does not depict a self-subsistent, immortal entity. Scripture teaches that only God has immortality (1 Timothy 6:16) and an immortal soul in humans would mean that they have innate immortality. . . Resurrection is God's supernatural answer to the problem of death. (1 Cor. 15:52–54).[54]

HERMENEUTICS

This may be a logical point at which to declare Seventh-day Adventist hermeneutical perspective. Hermeneutics, the study of methods for interpreting scripture or the science and art of the correct interpretation of the Bible, underlies comprehension in biblical interpretation. Therefore, any discussion of belief should contain a declaration of hermeneutical perspective and disclosure of methodology to aid the reader or hearer in accurate reception of the message.[55]

Ekkehardt Mueller observes, "A crucial and very practical issue today involves the question of which method should be employed to interpret Scripture, for interpretation is necessary, as pointed out even by Jesus (Luke 24:27)."[56] He affirms that Seventh-day Adventists rely on the historical-biblical method. He demonstrates that, "in contrast to most other approaches, the historical-biblical method acknowledges the self-testimony of Scripture and studies its phenomena."[57]

Alberto Timm asserts:

> The Christian church was originally built upon the hermeneutical platform of the Bible as it's on interpreter. Soon after the apostolate, however, the church began to move from that platform to accepting certain nonbiblical hermeneutical alternatives. The Scriptures came to be re-interpreted in many Christian circles from perspectives drawn from surrounding pagan cultures, cultural traditions, ecclesiastical authority, human reason, and even personal experiences. Major struggles and tensions arose between those who subscribe to such hermeneutical alternatives and those who try to re-orient the church back to its original hermeneutical platform.[58]

Sound hermeneutical principles for Bible interpretation are imperative. "The basic task of biblical hermeneutics is to determine what God has said in sacred Scripture and what it means for us today."[59] Mueller declares regarding the historical-biblical method:

- It accepts the claim that God revealed himself (1 Samuel 3:21).
- God entered into a relationship with the human authors of scripture (Amos 3:7; Ephesians 3:5).
- God also revealed propositional truth and communicated messages (Daniel 10:1; Titus 1:3).
- God inspired the human office to share these messages with others (2 Timothy 3:16; 1 Peter 1:10–12; 2 Peter 1:19–21).
- Then the inscripturated message is the Word of God (Mark 7:10–13).[60]

Ron du Preez, in his examination of methods for applying biblical ethics in interpreting scripture, sets up a fivefold task with guiding questions:

1. Supplication—the submissive task: What does the Spirit desire to teach us?

2. Observation—the descriptive task: What does the specific passage say?

3. Synthesization—the integrative task: What do the Scriptures, as a whole, say?

4. Interpretation—the hermeneutical task: What does this text mean for us?

5. Application—the pragmatic task: What then shall we do?[61]

A valid and reliable hermeneutical process requires "a sound system of principles that allows the text to speak for itself through *exegesis,* a procedure that consistently leads truth out of Bible texts. *Hermeneutics* refers to the machinery, and *exegesis* to the method, of biblical interpretation."[62] Gugliotto provides a tested six-step analytical procedure for exegesis found useful for personal growth, public teaching, or pulpit preaching.

1. *Contextual Analysis*: Locate the text in the larger body of revelation. Move through Old Testament to New Testament tracing the flow of the writer's thought, considering where and how the selected text fits into the full book—the immediate context.

2. *Structural Analysis*: Analyze the writer's literary style and determine the overall pattern. Identify characteristic features and categorize the passage by type of literature. Determine organization, views, main and supporting arguments, and the writer's series of connected thoughts. Mark the starting and ending points of the topics and themes.

3. *Verbal Analysis*: Focus on individual words and details to discover the writer's intentions. Explore the original setting

and the writer's language. Study unfamiliar words and decipher figures of speech and symbols. Define key terms within context.

4. *Cultural Analysis*: Investigate the historical-cultural background to the text using insights from history, anthropology, geography, and the environment. Seek to recover the original setting and immerse mentally in the writer's world.

5. *Theological Analysis*: Tie things together to build the whole story by expanding the range of study and relating the selected text to the rest of the Bible. Situate the passage in the broader context of the plan of salvation tracing it from promise to fulfillment to find its beginning and destination. Study its Old Testament roots or New Testament developments. Let earlier passages shed insight into later texts and later texts to understand earlier ones more fully.

6. *Homiletical Analysis*—Draw out the writer's meaning considering stylistic, physical, and psychological factors to connect that meaning in relevant ways to current context.[63]

SEVENTH-DAY ADVENTIST UNDERSTANDING OF CERTAIN DIFFICULT PASSAGES

While many passages appear to be clear on the nature of humankind and the state of the dead, others are less so and indeed can present problems of apparent contradictions. A few of these passages pose serious questions in light of Seventh-day Adventist views of the biblical portrayal of life and death. However, a review of the weight of evidence indicates harmony with biblical concepts of the wholeness of the human construct and rejection of inherent immortality of the soul.[64] Refer to official Seventh-day Adventist Church commentaries for extensive examinations of these passages. Here is provided only a cursory study of several passages for insight into the Seventh-day Adventist positions.

The following examples are excerpts, particularly from Niels-Erik Andreasen, from the *Handbook of Seventh-day Adventist Theology.*[65]

LUKE 23:43

Perhaps the passage cited most often in favor of immediate transport to Heaven at death is Luke 23:43, "Truly, I say to you, today you will be with me in Paradise." If read with a pause (or comma) after the words "Truly, I say to you," this verse states that Jesus invited the second thief on the cross to accompany him to paradise that day, implying immediate transport to heaven at death and perhaps continued soul existence after death. The meaning becomes altered dramatically if the pause (or comma) follows the word "today." In this case Jesus would promise, "Truly, I say to you today," indicating a present promise of a future entrance into heaven and eternal life.

Unfortunately, the oldest Greek manuscripts come without punctuation, so we must examine this verse in its context to determine its precise meaning. The intention of the verse is to offer the repentant thief on the cross salvation. Thus, there is no discussion of eternal reward or punishment, about entrance to heaven or hell. Instead, the immediate context is the subject of salvation on a day of extreme trouble for three men. In his reply Jesus offered immediate assurance of salvation to the repentant thief.

Jesus would not enter his kingdom that day or even the next day (John 20:17). He only wanted to give the repentant man assurance of salvation that very day. Thus, Luke 23:43 teaches assurance of salvation but not admission to the kingdom at the point of death.

2 CORINTHIANS 5:1–10 AND PHILIPPIANS 1:19–26

Next are two passages that pose a similar problem. They seem to favor death over life on the grounds that death would bring the faithful into a special, immediate relationship with their Lord. But closer examination of these texts reveals a different perspective, harmonious with the rest of the Bible.

The Apostle Paul divides human existence into three phases. The first, the present life in the flesh, is illustrated by an earthly tent in which we live and labor or by which we are clothed (2 Corinthians 5:1, 2; Philippians 1:22, 24). The second phase, death, is illustrated by nakedness, a state of being unclothed (2 Corinthians 5:3, 4). The apostle desires to avoid this phase through the experience of translation (1 Corinthians 15:51–57; 2 Corinthians 5:4), for nakedness represents an awkward condition in which he cannot benefit the church with his ministry (Philippians 1:24).

Elsewhere, Paul refers repeatedly to death as a sleep, confirming that death represents an inactive period during which one is unable to benefit the church, while not yet enjoying the presence of his Lord (1 Corinthians 15:6, 51; 1 Thessalonians 4:14). The third phase is represented by the life of resurrection and is illustrated by a building, a house not made with hands but made by God (2 Corinthians 5:1). Clearly this phase represents the apostle's ultimate aspiration, for it will bring him near the Lord (5:6, 8; Philippians 1:23).

Since this third phase is separated from the first earthly phase only by unconscious sleep with no sense of the passing of time for the deceased, it is natural for the text to juxtapose these two phases (Philippians 1:23). Only a resurrection from the dead or a translation from the living, not death itself, will bring the apostle to the last phase. For reasons already stated, he would rather not die (be unclothed) (2 Corinthians 5:9; Philippians 1:20–25). As for death, the state of nakedness, the apostle joins the biblical witness in decrying it and hoping for the day when "what is mortal may be swallowed up by life" (2 Corinthians 5:4).

1 THESSALONIANS 4:14

The troubling question here concerns those saints who have died and whom God will bring along with Christ. They will not accompany Christ from heaven to earth, but rather they will be raised from the grave to accompany Christ to heaven, as evidenced by the context (compare 1 Corinthians 6:14; 2 Corinthians 4:14). The dead in Christ shall rise first, then Jesus turns to those who are alive, the resurrected with him. Those who have died in the Advent hope they will not be left behind (1 Thessalonians 4:15) but will rise to meet the Lord first, even before he turns his attention to those who are still alive (4:16–17).

HEBREWS 12:23 AND REVELATION 6:9

These two texts speak of "spirits" and "souls" as though they were persons who had died. In the first is found the expression "spirits of just men made perfect" (Hebrews 12:23), and the second refers to souls under the altar, "slain for the word of God and for the witness they had borne" (Revelation 6:9). Together they illustrate two different uses of symbolic language.

In the first case, the apostle draws a distinction between two groups: the original Hebrews who came to Mount Sinai (Hebrews 12:18–19) and the Christian Hebrews to whom the epistle is addressed and who have come to Mount Zion (12:22). As with that first assembly at Mount Sinai (12:18–21), this second gathering at Mount Zion consists of God's saints, angels, humans, and Hebrew Christians, the firstborn of faith through the new covenant mediated by Jesus. They are not disembodied saints but real people, to whom the apostle appeals, "See that you do not refuse him who is speaking" (12:25).

The second passage symbolically describes events under the fifth seal (Revelation 6:9–11). It reports on the fate of Christian martyrs not yet avenged by God for their innocently spilled blood. Like the blood of innocent Abel crying to heaven for help (Genesis 4:10), so the blood of these martyrs, symbolically speaking, calls for God to attend to their case. The imagery of speaking blood is familiar in the Bible (compare Hebrews 12:24). It refers to the voice of the life represented by that blood, a life taken or given through the spilling of blood. The martyrs are told to wait (since two more seals remain to be opened) and to rest a little longer in their grave (Revelation 6:11). In this symbolic presentation of the resurrection hope held by those who died long ago, the dead play no active role but must patiently wait for the time established by God. This confirms the biblical understanding that the dead rest in the grave until called forth at the time of the resurrection.[66]

CONCLUSION:
THE SEVENTH-DAY ADVENTIST POSITION

Some understand human nature in terms of trichotomism, which divides it into body, soul, and spirit. Practically, trichotomism comes close to dichotomism (a form of dualism) because it divides human nature into parts, with at least one able to live independently of the others. Some associate dualism with Greek thought and monism with Jewish thought. Modern Christian thinking tends in the direction of wholism, ascribing salvation to the entire human being, not just a separate soul.[67]

In the mid-nineteenth century, a position with adherence to wholism, advanced by eighteenth-century clergymen and scholars on both sides of the Atlantic, was adopted by the young Seventh-day Adventist Church for several reasons: (1) It represents the biblical view, free of philosophical speculation and ecclesiastical tradition; (2) it was held by the early church, reemerging during and after the Reformation; (3) it affirms the familiar biblical portrayal of death as a sleeplike unconsciousness, rejecting the view of the soul's continued existence after death; (4) it supports the biblical teaching that immortality is not inherent in the nature of the soul, or bestowed at death, but granted only at the resurrection from the dead; (5) it underscores the New Testament emphasis on Christ as the only way to eternal life without consideration of any merits accruing to the soul following death.[68] Andreasen offers an apt conclusion: "The wholistic understanding of human nature, coupled with the teaching of conditional immortality, has been advocated consistently from the pulpit of the Seventh-day Adventist Church since its founding."[69]

NOTES

1. Philip Rodonioff, "Waking Up to Eternity," *Adventist World*, March 2012, 30–31.

2. Niels-Erik A. Andreasen, "Death: Origin, Nature, and Final Eradication," in *Handbook of Seventh-day Adventist Theology*, ed. Raoul Dederen (Hagerstown, MD: Review and Herald Publishing Association, 2001), 322–23.

3. John Dybdahl, ed., *Andrews Study Bible Notes* (Berrien Springs, MI: Andrews University Press, 2010), 1703.

4. Dybdahl, *Andrews Study Bible Notes*, 1703.

5. Oscar Cullmann, *Immortality of the Soul or Resurrection of the Dead?: The Witness of the New Testament* (Eugene, OR: Wipf and Stock Publishers, 2000).

6. Artur Stele, "Biblical Anthropology: Introduction and Challenges," in *What Are Human Beings That You Remember Them?*, ed. Clinton Whalen (Silver Spring, MD: Review and Herald Publishing Association, 2013).

7. Stele, "Biblical Anthropology," 2.

8. Stele, "Biblical Anthropology," 3.

9. Stele, "Biblical Anthropology," 4.

10. Stele, "Biblical Anthropology," 4.

11. Clinton Whalen, "Greek Philosophy, Judaism, and Biblical Anthropology," in Whalen, *What Are Human Beings That You Remember Them?*, 107–8.

12. James Arieti, "The Vocabulary of Septuagint Amos," *Journal of Biblical Literature* 93 (1974): 338–47.

13. Whalen, "Greek Philosophy, Judaism, and Biblical Anthropology," 113.

14. Andreasen, "Death: Origin, Nature, and Final Eradication," 337.

15. Andreasen, "Death: Origin, Nature, and Final Eradication," 336.

16. Andreasen, "Death: Origin, Nature, and Final Eradication," 336.

17. Andreasen, "Death: Origin, Nature, and Final Eradication," 337.

18. Jiri Moskala, "Eternal Punishment in Hell and the Immortality of the Soul: Overview of the Current Debate," in Whalen, *What Are Human Beings That You Remember Them?*, 96.

19. Felix Cortez, "Death and Future Hope in the Hebrew Bible," in Whalen, *What Are Human Beings That You Remember Them?*, 96.

20. Andreasen, "Death: Origin, Nature, and Final Eradication," 325.

21. Eriks Galenieks, *The Nature, Function, and Purpose of the Term [Sheol] in The Torah, Prophets, and Writings* (Berrien Springs, MI: Adventist Theological Society Publications, 2005), 612.

22. Richard Davidson, "The Nature of the Human Being from the Beginning: Genesis 1–11," in Whalen, *What Are Human Beings That You Remember Them?*, 30–31.

23. Andreasen, "Death: Origin, Nature, and Final Eradication," 337.

24. Børge Schantz and Steven Thompson, "Paul: Mission and Message," in *Biblical Missionaries, Seventh-day Adventist Adult Bible Study Guide*, 14 September 2015, 96.

25. Ray Ruppert, "What Happens Immediately After People Die—Soul Sleep," *Mediations*, October 16, 2015, https://ray-ruppert.blogspot.com/2015/10/what-happens-immediately-after-people_16.html.

26. Schantz and Thompson, "Paul: Mission and Message," 96.

27. "The Nature of Humanity," General Conference of the Seventh-day Adventist Church, https://www.adventist.org/en/beliefs/humanity/nature-of-humanity/.

28. F. LeRon Shults, *Reforming Theological Anthropology: After the Philosophical Turn to Relationality* (Grand Rapids, MI: Eerdmans, 2003), 175.

29. Richard Davidson, "Back to the Beginning: Genesis 1–3 and the Theological Center of Scripture," in *Christ, Salvation, and the Eschaton: Essays in Honor of Hans K. LaRondelle*, ed. Daniel Heinz, Jiri Moskala, and Peter M. Van Bemmelen (Berrien Springs, MI: Old Testament Publications, 2009), 11.

30. John Rankin, "Power and Gender at the Divinity School," in *Finding God at Harvard: Spiritual Journeys of Thinking Christians*, ed. Kelly Monroe (Grand Rapids, MI: Zondervan, 1996), 203.

31. Richard Davidson, "The Nature of the Human Being from the Beginning: Genesis 1–11," in Whalen, *What Are Human Beings That You Remember Them?*, 11.

32. Unless otherwise indicated, all scripture quotations are taken from the New King James Version.

33. Davidson, "Nature of the Human Being from the Beginning," 23.

34. Andreasen, "Death: Origin, Nature, and Final Eradication," 316.

35. Davidson, "Nature of the Human Being from the Beginning," 24.

36. Davidson, "Nature of the Human Being from the Beginning," 24.

37. Davidson, "Nature of the Human Being from the Beginning," 24.

38. Dybdahl, *Andrews Study Bible Notes*, 8 (notes for Genesis 2:7).

39. Davidson, "Nature of the Human Being from the Beginning," 25.

40. Francis D. Nichol, ed., *The Seventh-day Adventist Bible Commentary* (Silver Springs, MI: Review and Herald Publishing Association, 1978) 1:222.

41. Dybdahl, *Andrews Study Bible Notes*, 8 (notes for Genesis 2:7).

42. Nichol, *The Seventh-day Adventist Bible Commentary*, 1:222–23.

43. "Death and Resurrection," https://www.adventist.org/en/beliefs/restoration /death-and-resurrection/.

44. Andreasen, "Death: Origin, Nature, and Final Eradication," 337–38.

45. Andreasen, "Death: Origin, Nature, and Final Eradication," 326.

46. Andreasen, "Death: Origin, Nature, and Final Eradication," 324–25.

47. Andreasen, "Death: Origin, Nature, and Final Eradication," 345.

48. Andreasen, "Death: Origin, Nature, and Final Eradication," 342–45.

49. Andreasen, "Death: Origin, Nature, and Final Eradication," 318.

50. Andreasen, "Death: Origin, Nature, and Final Eradication," 318.

51. Andreasen, "Death: Origin, Nature, and Final Eradication," 333.

52. Andreasen, "Death: Origin, Nature, and Final Eradication," 333.

53. Dybdahl, *Andrews Study Bible Notes*, 1089 (notes for Ezekiel 37:1–14).

54. Kwabena Donkor, *Growing in Christ: The Way. The Truth. The Life* (Hagerstown, MD: Review and Herald Publishing Association, 2012), 86.

55. See Dederen, *Handbook of Seventh-day Adventist Theology* (Hagerstown, MD: Review and Herald, 2000).

56. Ekkehardt Mueller, "Guidelines for the Interpretation of Scripture," in *Understanding Scripture: An Adventist Approach*, ed. George W. Reid (Hagerstown, MD: Review and Herald Publishing Association, 2005), 111.

57. Muller, "Guidelines for the Interpretation of Scripture," 111.

58. Alberto Timm, "Historical Background of Adventist Biblical Interpretation," in Reid, *Understanding Scripture*, 1.

59. Hans K. LaRondelle, *The Israel of God in Prophecy: Principles of Prophetic Interpretation*, (Berrien Springs, MI: Andrews University Press, 1983), 7.

60. Ekkehardt Mueller, "Guidelines for the Interpretation of Scripture," 111.

61. Ron du Preez, "Interpreting and Applying Biblical Ethics," in Reid, *Understanding Scripture*, 286–87.

62. Lee J. Gugliotto, "Introduction," in *Handbook for Bible Study: A Guide to Understanding, Teaching, and Preaching the Word of God* (Hagerstown, MD: Review and Herald Publishing Association, 2000), 20.

63. Gugliotto, "Introduction," 20–21.

64. Andreasen, "Death: Origin, Nature, and Final Eradication," 326.

65. Dederen, *Handbook of Seventh-day Adventist Theology.*

66. Andreasen, "Death: Origin, Nature, and Final Eradication," 326–28.

67. Mueller, "Nature of the Human Being in the New Testament," 134.

68. Andreasen, "Death: Origin, Nature, and Final Eradication," 340.

69. Andreasen, "Death: Origin, Nature, and Final Eradication," 341.

Chapter 10

THY KINGDOM COME

ON EARTH AS IN HEAVEN

Luther Zeigler

The Reverend Luther Zeigler is a pastor and Episcopal chaplain (emeritus) at Harvard University in Cambridge, Massachusetts. He is a former president of the Harvard Chaplains and served as chair of the Board of Religious, Spiritual and Ethical Life at Harvard.

While I am a priest ordained in the Episcopal Church and educated and formed by the Anglican tradition, I do not pretend to represent our church's doctrine on this subject. I make this disclaimer in part because there is a diversity of perspectives within our tradition on Christian hope for resurrected life and in part because, if you know anything about Anglicanism, you probably know that we tend to be suspicious about doctrinal debates as such, at least when they are untethered from the experience of worship. We are a tradition guided by the maxim *lex orandi, lex credendi*—meaning, roughly, our praying shapes our believing. For most Episcopalians, as for most Anglicans, the *liturgy*—or the experience of the worshipping community—is at the heart of who we are as Christians, much more so than creeds, confessions, or any attempt to develop a systematic theological statement. Put simply, if you want to know what Episcopalians believe, come worship with us.

To some, this may sound like a bit of a dodge—that we Anglicans are either lacking in clear conviction or that we are so intent on holding together a compromise between Protestant and Catholic impulses that we end up finessing the precise contours of what we actually believe by hiding behind our liturgy. But let me suggest that something else a bit more principled may be going on here, and that is the insight that in the early church there was in fact a liturgical tradition before there was a common creed and before there was an officially sanctioned biblical canon. Common prayer, common Eucharistic practice, common song, and shared patterns of community life held the earliest Christian communities together more so than bare creeds or theology. And it is on this insight that we Anglicans hang much of our identity.

With this in mind, my initial temptation today was to answer the question "What do Episcopalians believe lies beyond the grave?" by actually walking you through the liturgy of the *Book of Common Prayer* for All Saints' Day, that feast day on our church calendar that points us toward the Christian hope for resurrected life. And if I had done so, we would have opened by singing together the great William Walsham How hymn "For All the Saints,"[1] set to the glorious music of Ralph Vaughn Williams. We would have heard lessons from the texts appointed for that day, like Revelation 21:1–6, which promises the re-creation of "a new heaven and a new earth," and the arrival of a New Jerusalem, a home for God among his creatures, where "He will dwell among them, and they shall be His people."[2] We then would have moved from the liturgy of the word to the liturgy of the table, experiencing anew the Eucharistic drama of Jesus Christ's life, death, resurrection, and ascension and how that sacramental rite empowers us to be kingdom bearers as we, his followers, are sent out into the world, sustained by an ultimate vision of resurrected life in God's kingdom, which was inaugurated by Jesus Christ but has yet to be fully realized. And along the way, we would have prayed, as we always do when we gather for worship, the words Jesus taught us to pray, saying, among other things, "Thy kingdom come. Thy will be done, on earth as it is in heaven" (Matthew 6:10).

Had I the time to do such an instructed Eucharist of our All Saints' Day liturgy, I am convinced you would have walked away from the exercise with a richly textured sense of what we Episcopalians believe lies beyond the grave, even as we may not always able to articulate that hope adequately in words. Happily for me, however, I am the grateful beneficiary of a masterful work on the subject of Christian hope by one of the great bishops in the Anglican Church, Tom Wright, whose book *Surprised by Hope: Rethinking Heaven, the Resurrection, and the Mission of the Church*[3] distills in a clear and fresh way what is expressed in our liturgy on the subject of Christian hope, and it is upon Bishop Wright's book that I will rely for much of what I will share with you today. In my humble opinion, Bishop Wright's book is one of the most important books written on the subject of this conference in the last several decades, and if you take nothing else away from my remarks today, I hope that you will at least be convinced by the time I'm finished that Bishop Wright's book is worth your study.

That leads me to my second qualification: I come to you neither as a biblical scholar nor as a professional theologian but rather as a humble university chaplain. The calling of a chaplain is, among other things, to be an interpreter of a tradition, a companion who walks alongside students who are desperately searching for meaning, purpose, and hope for their lives. What a good chaplain aims to do is to share with these students what his or her tradition has to offer in response to these big life questions, which is precisely why I am so enthusiastic about Bishop Wright's work on this subject because, as I shall try to suggest, one of the great virtues of his book is that he explains the Christian hope in a manner that is at once biblically grounded, theologically sophisticated, yet expressed in an entirely fresh and accessible way that speaks directly to the lived experience of our contemporary context.

With all that said, let me now summarize four key themes of Bishop Wright's book. My aim here is not to defend or argue for this conception of the Christian hope but rather, in keeping with the spirit of this ecumenical conference, merely to describe a vision of that hope that many of us in the Anglican communion find fresh and compelling.

THEME 1: THE CHRISTIAN HOPE IS FUNDAMENTALLY NOT ABOUT LEAVING THIS WORLD FOR ANOTHER ONE CALLED HEAVEN

Contrary to popular conceptions of the afterlife, and even to what most folks sitting in the pews may think, the Christian hope of a future life is not about dying and then leaving this world for some ethereal place in the sky called heaven. We know this first and foremost from Jesus's own preaching and teaching about God's kingdom, which consistently refers not to some postmortem destiny, not to an escape from this world into another one, but rather to a new age in which God will rule over a new heaven and a new earth. Our hope, according to Wright, is not going to heaven when we die but rather to the glorious day when God will make all things new and heaven and earth will merge in a newly created cosmos.

This is precisely the vision articulated in the twenty-first chapter of the Revelation to John, and it is what we pray for when we pray our Lord's Prayer and ask for God's kingdom to come on earth as it is in heaven. We should think of God's kingdom not as some separate sphere of existence but rather as a divine space-time reality that is interlocking with the course of human history, a divine reality that is already present by virtue of the resurrection and Jesus's ascension as Lord over all creation, but one that will not be fully realized until the end of time. "Salvation, then, is not 'going to heaven' but 'being raised to life in God's new heaven and new earth.'"[4]

THEME 2: THE CHRISTIAN HOPE IS FOR NEWLY EMBODIED LIFE, NOT A DISEMBODIED, SPIRITUAL EXISTENCE

So much popular thinking about the afterlife is rooted in a crude Platonic dualism that views human beings as made up of immortal souls or spirits tethered to mortal bodies. On this view, when we die, our immortal spirit leaves our decaying body for some other place called heaven. Yet this is not a view that finds much support in the New Testament. What we find in the New Testament, rather, is a conception of human identity that is an integrated mind-body-spirit unity, and the resurrection hope we have is for a newly re-created and embodied life.

The foundation for this hope for resurrected human life is, of course, the resurrected Christ himself. Jesus was raised bodily. The Gospel writers are keen to emphasize this point: the same Jesus who was physically present to his followers before his death, appears to them afterwards as an embodied presence, not some spiritualized vision. As Rowan Williams, our former archbishop of Canterbury, puts it: "In his ministry, Jesus created and sustained the community of his friends by speech and touch and the sharing of food; and so, after his resurrection, that community is sustained in the same way. It is not taken away from history, from matter, from bodies and words."[5] Our hope for resurrected life is, therefore, precisely this: a newly created, embodied life, as St. Paul goes to great lengths to explain in chapter 15 of his first letter to the Corinthians. The *telos* toward which the narrative arc of God's story is heading is a glorified, *incarnational* reality. As Bishop Wright neatly sums up this point, "The risen Jesus is both the *model* for the Christian's future body and the *means* by which it comes about."[6]

THEME 3: THE CHRISTIAN HOPE IS ABOUT COSMIC RENEWAL, NOT MERELY INDIVIDUAL SALVATION

One unfortunate legacy of post-Enlightenment thinking is an unhealthy preoccupation with the individual and the individual's own destiny. Yet, if we return to the biblical narrative, we see that the focus of the biblical story is not so much on personal salvation as it is the formation by God of a covenantal *people* to join him in his ultimate aim to renew the entire *cosmos*. Romans 8:19–24 is a key text here: as St. Paul so memorably expresses it, the whole "creation waits eagerly for the revealing of the sons of God," and our Christian "hope [is] that the creation itself also will be set free from its slavery to corruption and into the freedom of the glory of the children of God." To quote Wright, "What creation needs is neither abandonment nor evolution but rather redemption and renewal; and this is both promised and guaranteed by the resurrection of Jesus from the dead. This is what the whole world is waiting for."[7]

Preoccupied as we human beings are with our own individual futures, such self-absorption is but a reflection of a sinful narcissism that is rooted in a forgetfulness of God's much broader and more glorious redemptive purposes. The question of "what happens to me after death is *not* the major, central, framing question," argues Bishop Wright, adding:

> The New Testament, true to its Old Testament roots, regularly insists that the major, central, framing question is that of God's purpose of rescue and re-creation for the whole world, the entire cosmos. The destiny of individual human beings must be understood within that context—not simply in the sense that we are only part of a much larger picture but also in the sense that part of the whole point of being saved in the present is so that we can play a vital role (Paul speaks of this role in the shocking terms of being 'fellow workers with God') within that larger picture and purpose.

As he goes on to explain, this insight

> in turn makes us realize that the question of our own destiny, in terms of the alternatives of joy or woe, is probably the wrong way of looking at the whole question. The question ought to be, *How will God's new creation come?* and then, *How will we humans contribute to that renewal of creation and to the fresh projects that the creator God will launch in his new world?* The choice before humans would then be framed differently: are you going to worship the creator God and discover thereby what it means to become fully and gloriously human, reflecting his powerful, healing, transformative love into the world? Or are you going to worship the world as it is, boosting your corruptible humanness by gaining power or pleasure from forces within the world but merely contributing thereby to your own dehumanization and further corruption of the world itself?[8]

This understanding of resurrection as new creation thus points us forward, toward God's hope for a transformed future, rather than just looking backward at the resurrection as a mere historical fact. Bishop Wright puts it this way:

> The resurrection is not, as it were, a highly peculiar event within the *present* world (though it is that as well); it is, principally, the defining event of the *new* creation, the world that is being born with Jesus. If we are even to glimpse this new world, let alone enter it, we will need a different kind of knowing. . . . Hope is what you get when you suddenly realize that a different worldview is possible, a worldview in which the rich, the powerful, and the unscrupulous do not after all have the last word. The same worldview shift that is demanded by the resurrection of Jesus is the shift that will enable us to transform the world.[9]

THEME 4: THE CHURCH'S MISSION IS TO BECOME A COMMUNITY OF KINGDOM BEARERS

If the renewal of all creation is God's ultimate aim, then the church's role in the present is to embody an alternative order that stands as a sign of these redemptive purposes. This is made possible, of course, only by virtue of our baptism into the death and resurrection of Christ and our allegiance to the ascended Christ as Lord of all, which opens up a life of faith in God's continuing activity in our world and a hope for the promised new creation. "The revolutionary new world, which began in the resurrection of Jesus—the world where Jesus reigns as Lord, having won the victory over sin and death—has its frontline outposts in those who in baptism have shared his death and resurrection. The intermediate stage between the resurrection of Jesus and the renewal of the whole world is the renewal of human beings—you and me!—in our own lives of obedience here and now."[10]

Thus, we are not mere bystanders in this cosmic drama. On the contrary, since we have been created in the image of God, we are called to be his collaborators. "God intends his wise, creative, loving presence and power to be *reflected*—imaged, if you like—into his world *through* his human creatures. He has enlisted us to act as his stewards in the project of creation." That is, "through the work of Jesus and the power of the Spirit, [God] equips humans to help in the work of getting the project back on track." Some critics of Wright object that this sounds like works righteousness. But Wright is careful to insist that we are not the one's building the kingdom; that is purely God's doing. But God's loving purposes for us include allowing us to participate in his re-creation. So, as Wright puts it, "the objection about us trying to build God's kingdom by our own efforts, though it seems humble and pious, can actually be a way of hiding from responsibility, of keeping one's head well down when the boss is looking for volunteers."[11]

So, what then, does it look like to be a kingdom bearer? Again, we look to the resurrection for guidance, for in resurrecting his Son, God not only defeated sin and death but vindicated Christ's humanity as a sign of the new humanity toward which we are all called. Thus, every aspect of Jesus's life—his teaching, his welcoming, his healing, his sharing, his compassion, his forgiving, his community building, his prophetic challenges to unjust social arrangements—all of these dimensions of Christ's being in the world become for us a guide as to how we too may become kingdom bearers.

What is so inspiring about this aspect of the Christian hope is that we suddenly realize that everything we do in our day-to-day lives—from the smallest gestures of kindness to the noblest acts of bravery—are in fact a vital part of God's kingdom coming into reality. As Wright so eloquently phrases it:

> Every act of love, gratitude, and kindness; every work of art or music inspired by the love of God and delight in the beauty of his creation; every minute spent teaching a severely handicapped child to read or to walk; every act of care and nurture, of comfort and support, for one's fellow human beings and for that matter one's fellow nonhuman creatures; and of course every prayer, all Spirit-led teaching, every deed that spreads the gospel, builds up the church, embraces and embodies holiness rather than corruption, and makes the name of Jesus honored in the world—all of this will find its way, through the resurrecting power of God, into the new creation that God will one day make. That is the logic of the mission of God. God's recreation of his wonderful world, which began with the resurrection of Jesus and continues mysteriously as God's people live in the risen Christ and in the power of his Spirit, means that what we do in Christ and by the Spirit in the present is not wasted. It will last all the way into God's new world. In fact, it will be enhanced there.[12]

Let me conclude my remarks and this summary of Bishop Wright's vision of Christian hope by observing that this renewed understanding of the church's mission has important implications for evangelism as well. For too long, I think, evangelism has been framed in both individualistic and cognitive terms: as if the Christian project is to save individual souls through apologetics—that is, by seeking to persuade another person to believe this or that about Jesus Christ so that he or she might be saved. It's not that such a strategy is unworthy or wrong, but we might do well to ask whether a better way to build for the kingdom might be to focus more on compelling practices and patterns of resurrected living in community, rather than on private beliefs per se. Most of the young people I engage with on campus each day are much more moved—and ultimately persuaded—by authentically embodied expressions of Christian love, mercy, forgiveness, care, and the like, than they are by any set of claims. It's not more arguments that the Church needs, but more compelling examples of faithful people whose lives give quiet but powerful witness to the truth of the gospel and its promise of a new creation.

For many of us in the Anglican tradition, our faith is as much a way of life as it is a system of thought, as much a rhythm of life-giving practices as a collection of beliefs, as much a way of relating to others and the created world as a prescription for understanding it.

Long before Christianity became an institutionalized religion with creeds and confessional statements, it was known simply as "the Way" and was organized around a commitment to Jesus Christ as the divine embodiment of a new humanity and a new model for human community. In the early church, what differentiated Christians from others in the empire were primarily *practices* that pointed to the kingdom: the early Christians gave to the poor; cared for the sick; established communities without regard to class, social status, privilege, or gender; shared their resources without possessiveness; practiced hospitality to strangers and foreigners; repented of their sins with humility; sought and extended forgiveness; exercised an unrelenting ministry of reconciliation; prayed with regularity; and tried, individually and in community, to embody the fruits of a Spirit-filled life (love, joy, peace, patience, kindness, goodness, faithfulness, gentleness, and self-control), among the many other hallmarks of Christian living.

It's not that an understanding of scripture and statements of belief were unimportant to early Christians; certainly they were. The point is just that early Christians viewed their beliefs as inextricably bound up with the incarnational reality of seeking to live as the Body of Christ in the world. As Jesus himself said in the one parable he shared with his disciples about the Final Judgment, the famous parable of the sheep and the goats in Matthew 25, what will separate the sheep from the goats on the Day of Judgment will be less about our beliefs per se and more about whether and how we have cared for the least among us. By carefully articulating the foundations and life-giving shape of our hope in Christ, Bishop Wright has, I would respectfully submit, shown us how resurrected living here and now may give us the surest glimpse of the kingdom that lies beyond the grave.[13]

NOTES

1. The hymn may be found in *The Hymnal 1982, According to the Use of the Episcopal Church* (New York: Church Publishing, 1985), no. 287.
2. All scripture references in this article come from the New American Standard Bible.
3. N. T. Wright, *Surprised by Hope: Rethinking Heaven, the Resurrection, and the Mission of the Church* (New York: HarperOne, 2008). All citations in the text are to this edition.
4. Wright, *Surprised by Hope*, 198.
5. Rowan Williams, *Resurrection: Interpreting the Easter Gospel* (Cleveland: Pilgrim Press, 2002), 92–93.
6. Wright, *Surprised by Hope*, 149.
7. Wright, *Surprised by Hope*, 107.
8. Wright, *Surprised by Hope*, 184–85.
9. Wright, *Surprised by Hope*, 72–73, 75.
10. Wright, *Surprised by Hope*, 249.
11. Wright, *Surprised by Hope*, 207.
12. Wright, *Surprised by Hope*, 208–9.
13. For a particularly thoughtful review of Bishop Wright's book, and one that draws comparisons to Latter-day Saint theological perspectives on

the afterlife, see Robert L. Millet, "For Heaven's Sake: A Review of N. T. Wright's *Surprised by Hope*," *Religious Educator* 10, no. 3 (2009): 219–36.

INDEX

ABOUT THE EDITORS

Alonzo L. Gaskill is a professor in the Department of Church History and Doctrine, where he serves as a Richard L. Evans Fellow in the Office of Religious Outreach. He holds a bachelor's degree in philosophy, a master's degree in theology, and a PhD in biblical studies. He has taught at Brigham Young University since 2003. Before coming to BYU, he served in a variety of assignments within the Church Educational System—most recently as the director of the institute of religion at Stanford University. Gaskill is the author of twenty books and the editor or coeditor of five.

Since joining the Brigham Young University faculty in 1983, **Robert L. Millet** has served as dean of Religious Education, chair of the department of Ancient Scripture, director of the Religious Studies Center, and Richard L. Evans Professor of Religious Understanding. He is now professor emeritus of ancient scripture at BYU. He received his bachelor's and master's degrees in psychology from BYU and his PhD in religious studies from Florida State University. For decades Dr. Millet has been deeply involved in interfaith relations, including participation in formal academic dialogues with evangelical Christians, the Church of the Nazarene, and Community of Christ (formerly the Reorganized Church of Jesus Christ of Latter Day Saints). He is also a Distinguished Scholar with the John A. Widtsoe Foundation, with specific responsibilities for interfaith relations. He is the author or editor of more than seventy books and two hundred articles, book chapters, reviews, or encyclopedia entries, dealing mostly with the doctrine and history of The Church of Jesus Christ of Latter-day Saints and its relationship to other faiths.